Understanding
YOUR
BIBLE
in 15 Minutes a Day

Understanding
YOUR
BIBLE
in 15 Minutes a Day

DARYL AARON

FALL RIVER PRESS

New York

FALL RIVER PRESS

New York

An Imprint of Sterling Publishing
387 Park Avenue South
New York, NY 10016

ISBN 978-1-4351-5005-8

Use of italics for emphasis in Scripture quotations is the author's.

Unless otherwise noted, Scripture quotations are from the Holy Bible, New
International Version®. NIV®. Copyright © 1973, 1978, 1984, 2011 by Biblica, Inc.™
Used by permission of Zondervan. All rights reserved worldwide. www.zondervan.
com. Scripture marked NIV is taken from the HOLY BIBLE, NEW INTERNATIONAL
VERSION®. Copyright © 1973, 1978, 1984 Biblica. Used by permission of Zondervan.
All rights reserved. Scripture quotations marked NASB are from the New American
Standard Bible®, copyright © 1960, 1962, 1968, 1971, 1973, 1975, 1977, 1995 by
The Lockman Foundation. Used by permission. Scripture quotations marked NET
are from the NET BIBLE®, copyright © 2003 by Biblical Studies Press, LLC.
www.netbible.com. Used by permission. All rights reserved. Scripture
quotations marked KJV are from the King James Version of the Bible.

Distributed in Canada by Sterling Publishing
c/o Canadian Manda Group, 165 Dufferin Street
Toronto, Ontario, Canada M6K 3H6
Distributed in the United Kingdom by GMC Distribution Services
Castle Place, 166 High Street, Lewes, East Sussex, England BN7 1XU
Distributed in Australia by Capricorn Link (Australia) Pty. Ltd.
P.O. Box 704, Windsor, NSW 2756, Australia

For information about custom editions, special sales, and premium and
corporate purchases, please contact Sterling Special Sales at 800-805-5489
or specialsales@sterlingpublishing.com.

Manufactured in the United States of America

2 4 6 8 10 9 7 5 3 1

www.sterlingpublishing.com

This book is dedicated to my parents,
Ralph and Ruth Aaron, from whom I have received
a precious spiritual heritage, including a love
for the Word of God and the God of the Word,
for which I will be forever grateful.

Contents

Introduction 9

Introduction

Why would anyone want to read the Bible? It's old, it's huge, and sometimes it's really hard to understand. On the other hand, it makes several amazing and intriguing claims. It claims to be the Word of God (such as in 1 Thessalonians 2:13). It claims to be truth (John 17:17). It claims to be "alive and active" (Hebrews 4:12); "living and enduring" (1 Peter 1:23). If these claims are valid, the question should be: Who *wouldn't* want to read the Bible?

But regardless of these claims, the Bible is still old, big, and challenging, and therefore it is a daunting book to dive into and start reading. It is my hope that the book you're holding will aid you in overcoming some of these obstacles.

We know that most people's schedules are tight, and we certainly don't want to take away from time you would spend reading the Bible itself. Therefore, we've organized this book into forty short chapters that can easily be read in only fifteen minutes each. You'll be amazed how much you can learn in such a short amount of time! Each chapter answers a single question, such as "Who wrote the New Testament?" or "How is the Old Testament organized?" I've tried to keep the style friendly and light, such as by including Fun Facts along the way.

The chapters cover a broad spectrum of topics designed for everyone from those who have never picked up a Bible to more seasoned readers, looking for an enjoyable refresher. Several of the chapters revolve around the fact that the Bible is historical literature. That means the individual books that make up the Bible were written by a variety of authors a long time ago. They were written for specific people in a specific time and place. Everything we can learn about these people and places will help us understand these books better, so we will discuss issues of authorship, audience, and historical and geographical settings in order to get our bearings.

The Bible is also made up of a variety of types of literature—prose, poetry, and more. We will examine these genres and briefly summarize what can be found in each type of literature or section of the Bible.

We also must not forget that this ancient literature has survived for thousands of years and found its way into our culture and language. How did that happen? We will look at the original languages of the Bible, how those languages were translated into other languages (specifically English), and why certain books made it into the Old and New Testaments and why others did not.

As mentioned above, the Bible can be challenging. But if it really is the Word of God, then we should not expect it to be easy to understand, any more than God himself is easy to understand. But we will survey some basic methods and principles that can be used by any reader in order to better understand the Bible and what it means.

We will also investigate some of the claims mentioned above. Is there good evidence within the Bible as well as outside the Bible that it really is the Word of God, that it really is true and trustworthy, and that it really is dynamic and life-changing? And if it really is life-changing, how can we use it to change our lives for the better? We will be introduced to some ways to get the Word of God into us so that it can do what God wants it to (for example, Bible reading schedules, memorization, and meditation).

I have written this book from an evangelical perspective. That means I am convinced of and committed to basic ideas such as these: The Bible is what it claims to be—the very Word of God, without error, completely true and trustworthy; Jesus Christ is who he claimed to be—fully and eternally God as well as fully human; Jesus Christ really did die historically and physically, really was resurrected historically and physically, and he really is coming back to earth physically and visibly; and finally, faith in Jesus Christ is the only way for sinners like all of us to be accepted by God and enjoy his presence forever.

Because this is a book about the Bible, I have placed a lot of biblical texts into each chapter. Some of the more important ones are quoted. Unless otherwise noted, these quotations are from the New International Version 2011. For the most part, however, biblical references are simply cited to support or illustrate the points of discussion in each chapter. To gain the greatest benefit from this book, I would encourage you to look up these references, read them, and consider how they support the discussion.

It is my hope that this book will encourage and help you get into the Book—the Bible, the Word of God—in order to get to know its author, God himself, who, above all things, is worthy to be known.

Why Should I Read the Bible?

Second Timothy 3:16 contains one of the most important statements in the Bible about where the Bible came from and what it is: "All Scripture is God-breathed." As we will discuss further in a later chapter, this means that the Bible is from God and is indeed the very Word of God. That makes the Bible the most important book that has ever been written. But what will reading the Bible do for you? If we continue reading 2 Timothy 3:16–17, we'll find a helpful purpose statement for the Bible: "All Scripture is God-breathed and is [therefore] useful for teaching, rebuking, correcting and training in righteousness, *so that* the servant of God may be thoroughly equipped for every good work."

Of the four terms at the end of verse 16, the first and last are positive—*teaching* and *training in righteousness*. The middle two are negative—*rebuking* and *correcting*. All of these revolve around the important issue of truth. We can think of truth as that which conforms to God, his thinking, and his way of doing things. Teaching and training refer to leading the reader of the

Bible into truth, whereas rebuking and correcting refer to turning someone away from error and back to truth. This was a major concern of Paul as he wrote this letter to Timothy. A few verses later he writes, "For the time will come when people will not put up with sound doctrine" (4:3). *Sound doctrine* means "healthy truth." Being led into error or false teaching is an ongoing threat to Christians and all people.

The Bible is to be used to prevent this from happening and to lead people further and deeper into God's truth "so that the servant of God [the Christian—the one who has trusted in Jesus Christ as Savior], may be thoroughly equipped for every good work" (3:17). This means that God works through his Word, the Bible, to lead people into truth *so that* they can do everything that he calls them to do. That makes the Bible a crucial God-given resource for us to use so that we can please him.

What kind of truth does the Bible guide us into? The first and most important truth is about God—who he is and what he has done. God has done everything that he has done, including giving us the Bible, in order to be known as he really is. This is of utmost importance because God is the most important being that can be known. To not know God is infinitely tragic. God himself said, "Let not the wise boast of their wisdom or the strong boast of their strength or the rich boast of their riches, but let the one who boasts boast about this: that they have the understanding to know me, that I am the Lord" (Jeremiah 9:23–24). There is *nothing* more important than knowing God in the right way. This leads to truth in *everything* else.

The Bible also leads us into truth about the world—where it came from and why it is here. The world did not just happen; it was intentionally created by God (Genesis 1:1). Therefore, there is a purpose for its existence: to reveal the God of creation and to honor him. "The heavens declare the glory of God; the skies proclaim the work of his hands" (Psalm 19:1).

The Bible leads us into truth about ourselves—where we came from and why we are here. Humans, too, did not just happen to come into existence as an "accident" of evolution. Like the world, humans were intentionally created by God. We have a purpose for existence, and it is the same purpose as the universe in general—to honor and glorify God. This is the significance of being created in the "image of God" (Genesis 1:26–27). God created humans to be mirrors that reflect his being and glory (Isaiah 43:7). That, too, is why we are commanded to do everything for the glory of God (1 Corinthians 10:31).

The Bible also leads us into truth about the situation in which we find ourselves and the world—sinful and dysfunctional. Due to the unwillingness of humans to obey God and fulfill the purpose for which we were created, we are now characterized as "sinful," which is another way of saying we are guilty. "For all have sinned and fall short of the glory of God" (Romans 3:23). Even more so, we are no longer even *able* to obey God and fulfill this purpose; we are dysfunctional. "The mind governed by the flesh is hostile to God; it does not submit to God's law, nor can it do so" (Romans 8:7). This dysfunction extends to the whole creation. "For the creation was subjected to frustration, not by its own choice, but by the will of the one who subjected it" (Romans 8:20; see also Genesis 3:17).

The Bible also leads us into truth about the solution to the problem in which we and the world find ourselves—Jesus Christ and his work of salvation. Paul puts it succinctly in Titus 2:14: "[Christ Jesus] gave himself for us to redeem us from all wickedness and to purify for himself a people that are his very own, eager to do what is good." The work of Christ also fixes the wrongs that sin has done to the whole of God's creation. "The creation itself will be liberated from its bondage to decay and brought into the freedom and glory of the children of God" (Romans 8:21).

If we know all of this truth and *believe* it to be true, the result is that we will be "born again." First Peter 1:23 says, "For you have been born again, not of perishable seed, but of imperishable, *through the living and enduring word of God.*" This means that God transforms people through his Word. They are very different than they were before. That is why they are now "thoroughly equipped for every good work" (2 Timothy 3:17) and able to fulfill the purpose for which they have been created: to glorify God and to enjoy Him forever.[1] There is no greater good for humans than this. "I delight greatly in the LORD; my soul rejoices in my God. For he has clothed me with garments of salvation and arrayed me in a robe of his righteousness" (Isaiah 61:10). Is it any wonder that the psalmist said, "How sweet are your words to my taste, sweeter than honey to my mouth!" (Psalm 119:103).

COMMERCIAL FACT

Many of the bestsellers today are self-help books. But the bestseller of all time is the Bible, which, amazingly, fits into the opposite category—it's a non-self-help book. The Bible teaches us that we cannot help ourselves, but God can. He freely offers all the help we need. What will reading the Bible do for us? Among many other things, it will teach us to trust in and depend upon God alone. "Trust in the LORD with all your heart and lean not on your own understanding; in all your ways acknowledge him, and he will make your paths straight" (Proverbs 3:5-6 NIV 1984).

Where in the Bible
Can I Learn (and Teach Others)
How to Be Saved?

Your relationship with God, without a doubt, is the most important issue in your life. Much of the Bible addresses this vital matter. Even though many topics presented in the Bible are complex and challenging to comprehend, this particular issue is clear and easily understood by anyone open to what the Bible has to say. In this chapter, I provide an abundance of passages in the Bible that will both answer the question in the chapter's title and also show how often and how clearly these matters are discussed in Scripture. I would encourage you to read these verses for yourself.

The Intention. God, the ultimate being and creator of all things, created humans in his own image, which means we are like God in certain ways (Genesis 1:27). God intended humans to enjoy a close, intimate relationship with him and to reflect his character (his "glory") into the world that God had made. But God also wanted humans to do this gladly and willingly, so he created them with moral responsibility. This meant human beings could freely choose whether they wanted what God wanted, or something else.

The Problem. Things went horribly wrong very quickly. The sad story, recorded in Genesis 3 and called *the fall,* is about the first humans, Adam and Eve. They demonstrated that they desired other things more than God and chose to disobey God. As a result, sin and its constant companion, death, came into the world that God had created (Romans 5:18). *Sin* refers to anything that is contrary to God or his will. This is the condition of all people born since the time of Adam. "For all have sinned and fall short of the glory of God" (Romans 3:23; read also Paul's intense description of this state in Romans 3:9–18). This means that as a result of sin, we cannot do what God created us to do, namely, reflect his glory. We are now like carnival mirrors that reflect a distorted and twisted image. Also, "the wages of sin is death" (Romans 6:23; also Ephesians 2:1–3). *Death* means "separation." So death resulting from sin means that we have been separated from God and cannot enjoy the intimate relationship with God for which we were created. But what is worse, now God is angry with us and we face his condemnation (John 3:18, 36; Romans 1:18; 2:5). The destiny of all people who remain in this condition is eternal separation from God in a terrible place of punishment, which the Bible calls hell. Being in this condition of sin also means that sinners cannot do anything about it; sin is a part of our nature (Ephesians 2:3), and we cannot change that any more than we can change the fact that we are human. As sinners, we have a huge problem before God, and we cannot do anything to solve the problem, because we *are* the problem (Romans 8:7–8).

The Solution. God is just—which means he always does what is right and fair—and he must deal justly with sinful people. But he is also a God of love (1 John 4:8, 16), and he continues to love even sinful people. Motivated by this love, God did for us, as sinners, what we could not do for ourselves: he sent his own Son, Jesus

Christ, who is fully God, to take on a human nature like our own in order to pay the penalty for our sin. He experienced the punishment that we should have experienced and died in our place (Mark 10:45; John 1:29; 3:16; Romans 5:8; 1 Timothy 1:15; 1 Peter 3:18; 1 John 3:16; 4:9–10). Jesus did die, but he was also resurrected, showing that his Father had accepted his sacrificial death and was pleased with it (Romans 1:4; 4:25). The plan worked! This is the gospel, or good news (1 Corinthians 15:3–4).

This is what God has done for us as sinners through his Son, Jesus. What must we do? The Bible's answer is straightforward: Believe (John 3:15–18; 5:24; 20:31; Acts 16:30–31; Romans 10:9–10). To our problem of sin, God offers the solution as a gift. This is what the term *grace* means—something that is free, unearned, or undeserved (Romans 3:24; Ephesians 2:8–9). But as is true of any gift, it does us no good unless we receive it (John 1:12); only then does it become our own. Belief, or faith, is the God-given way we receive his gift of salvation through Jesus Christ.

It is important to understand, however, that this is more than an intellectual thing. To believe or have faith that results in salvation means to trust in, depend upon, or rely on Christ. We must totally depend upon what God has done for us through Jesus and not at all on anything that we do for God (Romans 3:27–28; 4:4–5; Galatians 2:16; Ephesians 2:8–9; 2 Timothy 1:9; Titus 3:5). It is a one-way transaction—God offers a free gift, and we receive it by faith. Think of a person who is drowning. Unless someone offers help, this person will die. And someone does offer help by throwing a life preserver to the person. But in order to be saved, the person must know what it is (a life preserver) and that it is actually there and not just a wishful thought of their dying imagination. But the person is not rescued until he grabs on to the life preserver and hangs on for dear life. To be saved, we must know what the gospel is, believe it to be true, and then rely or depend upon Jesus exclusively for our eternal destination.

The Result. When we believe in this way, all kinds of things happen. We are saved (Acts 16:31). We are forgiven for all of our sins (Acts 3:19; Ephesians 1:7; Colossians 2:13). We are declared "not guilty" by God ("justified" in Romans 3:24–26). We become saints, or "holy people" (2 Corinthians 1:1; Philippians 1:1). We are given eternal life (John 3:16). We regain a relationship with God and become a part of his kingdom (Colossians 1:13) and even his family (Romans 8:15–16; Ephesians 1:5). We are redeemed, or set free from, the power of sin (Titus 2:14). This does not mean that we will no longer sin. It does, however, mean that we now desire to please God and are able not to sin (Romans 6:7–14). We can also do this through the help of the Holy Spirit who now lives within us (Romans 8:5–11; 1 Corinthians 3:16; Galatians 5:16–25). These are just a few of the amazing things that God gives us as a part of the gift of salvation.

So how can a person be saved? First, acknowledge your sin and helplessness to God. Second, acknowledge your total dependence upon what Jesus has accomplished through his death and resurrection. And finally, accept God's gift of salvation. The best way to do this is by talking to God through prayer.

COMFORTING FACT

The Bible promises that "everyone who calls on the name of the Lord will be saved" (Romans 10:13). This is not something that we need to be unsure about. If we are truly depending on Jesus for our salvation, the Word of God assures us that we will be saved.

Does the Bible Tell One Overall Story?

The Bible does indeed tell a story. Not only is it a true story, it is the most significant story that will ever be told. It is fundamentally about God and his work. Some of the story has already happened; some of it is happening now; some of it is yet to happen, but it most certainly will happen.

The story begins with creation, which is the beginning of everything other than God himself (Genesis 1–2). Here we see an amazingly powerful God who simply spoke and things happened (1:3, 6, 9ff.), and an amazingly wise God who made everything in the best possible way and described it as "very good" (1:31). The pinnacle of creation was the man and woman created in his own image (1:27). He gave them jobs to do: "Be fruitful and increase in number; fill the earth and subdue it" (1:28), and moral responsibility—a single rule to obey (2:17).

Genesis 3 records the next step in the story, when God's image-bearers failed in their moral responsibility, and sin and evil became a defining part of the story. This is often called *a fall*. There were monumental consequences of the fall: death, a distorted and dysfunctional creation, and banishment from the garden of Eden (3:14–24). Sinful humanity became alienated from its creator God and subject to his wrath and condemnation, described in stunning terms in Romans 1:18–32.

Genesis 4–11 describes the growth and spread of sin and how God initially dealt with it, which he had to because he is holy and just. "The LORD saw how great the wickedness of the human race had become on the earth, and that every inclination of the thoughts of the human heart was only evil all the time" (6:5). Two divine judgments resulted: the flood (chapters 6–8) and the scrambling of human languages (chapter 11).

Genesis chapter 12 is a major turning point in the story, when God focuses his attention on one man—Abram, later called Abraham—and his descendants as the means by which God will deal with human sinfulness. An important subplot in the story is seen here—God entering into covenant relationships with people. The term *covenant* describes a formal relationship between two parties, and in this and other biblical covenants, the two parties are a human (and his descendants) and God himself. We might call this a contract. A covenant can be conditional or unconditional. When God chose Abraham, he initiated an *unconditional,* no-strings-attached covenant with him, known as the Abrahamic covenant (12:1–3). God promised Abraham that he would have many descendants (known as God's "chosen people"; we know them today as Jews), a land for those descendants to live in forever, and blessings for Abraham personally, his descendants, and all peoples on the earth through Abraham (12:3). These covenant promises continue to ripple through the rest of the book of Genesis, and indeed the whole Bible.

The rest of Genesis tells about how God brought Abraham to the Promised Land; how his descendants began to grow through his son and grandson, Isaac and Jacob; how these descendants multiplied into twelve tribes through the sons of Jacob; and how God temporarily led them to Egypt, where he would protect them and continue to multiply them, even through an extended time of slavery.

The book of Exodus tells us about one of the greatest events in the history of God's chosen people. Through a series of disasters inflicted upon the Egyptians, God led his people out of their enslavement. This great event, called *the exodus*, became a defining part of their heritage; it is to Jews what the Fourth of July is to Americans. He then led them into the wilderness, declared them to be the *nation* of Israel, declared himself to be their King, and, as any king would do, gave them his laws to obey. These laws form another important biblical covenant, known as the Mosaic or Sinai covenant, also known as "the Law." But this covenant, unlike all the others, was *very* conditional. Essentially, God was saying, "*If* you obey me, I will bless you; *if* you disobey me, I will curse you."

God eventually brought the Israelites back to the Promised Land, as recorded in the book of Joshua, and established them there. The rest of the history of the Old Testament can be briefly but accurately summarized as the ongoing sinfulness and rebellion of God's people and how God continued to deal with that rebellion through judgment and discipline (the books of Judges through 2 Chronicles).

There were bright spots in this dismal history when there would be a spiritual turnaround for a while, for example, through Samuel, King Hezekiah, Ezra, and others. One very bright spot in Israel's history is King David. God chose him to be the king of his people, and he became a great king because God greatly blessed him (2 Samuel 5:10). Another covenant is initiated here—the Davidic covenant. God *unconditionally* promised David that he would have many descendants and that among them there would be an eternal throne or kingdom (2 Samuel 7:5–16).

Due to Israel's ongoing sin, God eventually did what he had said he would do—he expelled them from the Promised Land (2 Kings 17, 25). They lived in exile for seventy years (Daniel 9:2). But after that, God brought them back to the Promised Land, just as he had promised to do (the books of Ezra and Nehemiah). In all of this, God was demonstrating his faithfulness to his covenant promises.

The Story continues in the New Testament with the birth, life, death, and resurrection of Jesus Christ, as told in the Gospels. He was the fulfillment of the promise of God, announced by Old Testament prophets, that he would send the "anointed one," the Messiah, to deliver God's people. This Promised One was none other than God himself who became man. His death was what was being portrayed through the sacrifice of animals in the Old Testament. God's Son was the perfect and final sacrifice for the sin of humanity. His message and that of his followers is the gospel, or good news: place your faith in Jesus and receive the forgiveness of sins and enjoy the blessings of God forever (e.g., John 3:15–16, 36; Acts 16:30–31).

This was also the fulfillment of another promise of God in the Old Testament and another divine covenant—the new covenant. It was announced by Jeremiah (31:31–34), but it was initiated by the death of Jesus (Luke 22:20; Hebrews 8–9; 12:24). The great *unconditional* divine promise in this covenant is that, through Jesus Christ, God does for sinful people what they cannot do for themselves, which is live holy lives in order to be pleasing to God. All of those who place their faith in Jesus Christ are a part of this covenant.

The New Testament book of Acts records how the followers of Jesus spread out and proclaimed this message. Many people believed it, but many others continued to reject it and persecuted those who believed it; those who believed were gathered into churches to be taught and encouraged in their faith.

We are in this part of the Story now. The gospel continues to be proclaimed around the world to "all nations," as Jesus commanded (Matthew 28:19–20), and the followers of Jesus continue to grow, individually and corporately.

There is more to the Story yet to happen. When Jesus left the earth, he promised to return (John 14:1–3). The Old Testament prophets and the New Testament authors spoke about this often (for example, Zechariah 14; 1 Thessalonians 4:13–5:11). When he does return, he will come to defeat those who hate him, judge the unrighteous, deliver his own people once and for all, and reign on the earth. The book of Revelation describes this, though with much imagery and symbolism.

Note how the end of the Story (Revelation) relates back to the beginning (Genesis). The new heaven and the new earth restore God's creation to its original goodness (Revelation 21:1). Rather than being alienated from God through sin, the righteous will live with God forever (Revelation 21:3–7). Rather than being barred from the tree of life, the righteous have constant access to it (Revelation 22:1–2). Rather than being under the curse, the curse will forever be removed (Revelation 22:3).

When Jesus returns, he will be the complete fulfillment of all God's covenant promises. In fulfillment of the Abrahamic covenant, he is the descendant of Abraham, and through him all the peoples on earth will be blessed. In fulfillment of the Mosaic covenant, he is the only human to perfectly obey all of God's commands. In fulfillment of the Davidic covenant, he will reign on earth on the throne of King David. And in fulfillment of the new covenant, all of his people will please God through their obedience to him.

The Story is about God and his faithfulness to his covenant promises. All those who are right with God through Jesus Christ will enjoy those promises forever and ever. Is there any wonder that the longing of God's people is "Come, Lord Jesus"? (Revelation 22:20).

FUN FACT

As the title of a 1965 film about the gospel declared, this is indeed *The Greatest Story Ever Told.*

What Is the Main Theme
of the Bible?

Trying to determine the main theme of the Bible is tricky business. It is like asking, "What is the most important thing about God?" There are no easy answers to these kinds of questions, but one very important theme of the Bible, perhaps *the* most important theme, is Jesus Christ. Most people would recognize this as true for the New Testament, but for the Old Testament? Absolutely. The Old Testament anticipates or foreshadows Jesus Christ. The New Testament fulfills the Old Testament by revealing Jesus Christ.

This begins at creation. Genesis 1:1 says, "God created the heavens and the earth." But the New Testament clarifies that the Son of God specifically was the agent, or cause, of creation (John 1:1–3, 10; 1 Corinthians 8:6; Hebrews 1:2). Colossians 1:16 is especially relevant here: "For in [Christ, the Son of God] all things were created . . . all things have been created through him and for him." This and other biblical texts indicate that not only is he the agent of creation, he is the very goal of creation: "All things have been created . . . *for* him." That means we live in a *Son-centered universe.*[1] Everything in it is about Jesus Christ. So the theme of Christ starts in Genesis 1:1: He is the beginning (and goal) of creation.

He is also mentioned in the consequences of the fall. God said to the serpent/tempter, "I will put enmity between you and the woman, and between your offspring and hers; he will crush your head, and you will strike his heel" (Genesis 3:15). This has come to be known as the *protoevangelium,* or first proclamation of the gospel. The "he" seems to refer to Jesus, and the "you" seems to refer to Satan. Satan would "wound" Jesus through the crucifixion, but Jesus would inflict a fatal blow on Satan and evil by the crucifixion (see, for example, Colossians 2:15; Hebrews 2:14; 1 John 3:8).

The flood in the days of Noah was God's judgment and symbolic of divine judgment in general. First Peter 3:20–21 shows Noah's ark as a symbol of salvation from the judgment of God, through Jesus Christ. Another Old Testament symbol of salvation in Christ is the bronze snake that provided healing for the people bitten by snakes (Numbers 21:6–9). John 3:14–15 says, "Just as Moses lifted up the snake in the wilderness, so the Son of Man must be lifted up, that everyone who believes may have eternal life in him."

As noted in the previous chapter, Jesus Christ is the ultimate fulfillment of the Old Testament covenants. He is a descendant of Abraham and will bring blessing to "all peoples on earth" (Genesis 12:3). He is also a descendant of David and will reign on the throne of David forever. The death of Christ initiated the new covenant, and all who believe in Christ are members of that eternal covenant.

The great exodus event is also primarily about Jesus Christ. In 1 Corinthians 5:7, he is referred to as "our Passover lamb [who] has been sacrificed." As God redeemed his chosen people from their enslavement in Egypt through the event known as the Passover, so God, through Christ, redeems his people from their enslavement to sin.

Christ also fulfilled the Mosaic covenant, also known as "the Law" (Matthew 5:17). He is the only person who ever did or will perfectly obey all of God's laws. But Christ is also seen in this covenant in other ways. Most explicitly, all of the animal sacrifices that were mandated in the law anticipate, or symbolize, the final and perfect sacrifice of Jesus (Hebrews 9:12–14; 10:4).

Another mandate in the Law was the building of the tabernacle. The Hebrew word for tabernacle means "dwelling place." It symbolized God's intention to dwell among his people (Exodus 25:8–9). This intention was fulfilled when he, through his Son, not only came to dwell among his people but actually became one of them in order to share their humanity. John 1:14 says, "The Word [Christ] became flesh and made his dwelling [tabernacled] among us." The furnishings of the tabernacle also symbolize Christ (these are described in Exodus 37–40). There was a table where twelve loaves of fresh bread would be placed daily; Jesus said, "I am the bread of life" (John 6:35). There was a lampstand to provide light in the tabernacle; Jesus said, "I am the light of the world" (John 8:12). The sacrifices offered on the altar and the sacrificial blood taken into the Most Holy Place symbolize the sacrifice and the blood of Christ that allows sinful people into the very presence of a holy God (Hebrews 9:3–14).

Christ is even anticipated in some of the holy days that were a part of the Law. As already noted, the Passover Feast (Leviticus 23:5) is about Christ. The Feast of Firstfruits (Leviticus 23:9–14) anticipates Christ who is the firstfruit of the resurrection (1 Corinthians 15:20). The Day of Atonement (Leviticus 23:26–32) anticipates the final atonement for sin made by Jesus (Hebrews 9:28).

Jesus Christ is also seen in the three offices of the Old Testament: prophet, priest, and king. The many prophets of the Old Testament looked forward to the greatest prophet, Jesus (Hebrews 1:1–2). The priests established in the Law anticipated Jesus Christ, who is the great high priest (Hebrews 4:14; 5:5–6). The kings of God's people, especially King David, anticipated Jesus Christ, the King of kings (1 Timothy 6:14–15).

The Old Testament prophets also anticipated the coming of the Messiah, Jesus Christ. Probably the best summary of these many texts, as well as what we have already seen and more, is what Jesus himself said to his disciples: "Everything must be fulfilled that is written *about me* in the Law of Moses, the Prophets and the Psalms [the entire Old Testament]" (Luke 24:44; see also Luke 24:27). The theme of the Old Testament is Jesus Christ.

As we come to the New Testament, this theme becomes clear and explicit. The following is a brief summary of what the New Testament says about him.

Not only has he created all things and is the goal of all things, "He is before *all* things, and in him *all* things hold together" (Colossians 1:17). He sustains *all* things by his powerful word (Hebrews 1:3). He has reconciled *all* things to himself (Colossians 1:20). In him are "hidden *all* the treasures of wisdom and knowledge" (Colossians 2:3). He is the judge of *all* people (John 5:24–30). He is the *only* way to the Father (John 14:6). He is head of *all* things (Ephesians 1:22). He is supreme over *all* things (Colossians 1:18). He is heir of *all* things (Hebrews 1:2). He has authority over *all* things (Matthew 28:18). For all of these reasons and much, much more, he has been glorified and exalted by God and must be glorified and exalted by *all* people (Philippians 2:9–11).

LIFE-PRIORITIZING FACT

Jesus Christ is "the Alpha and the Omega, the First and the Last, the Beginning and the End" (Revelation 22:13). This means that every aspect of our lives every day that we live should be oriented toward Jesus Christ.

Where Do the
Events of the Bible
Take Place?

The events of the Bible not only take place at a real time in history but also at real locations on earth. Understanding the setting is important and helpful for at least two reasons. First, getting a better sense of the geography helps clarify things for readers today who don't know what the original readers knew. They lived in that geographical setting, and we do not. We tend to superimpose our own geographical setting onto biblical events. I grew up in Iowa, so I naturally assumed that the setting of these stories was flat prairie as far as the eye could see (which is hardly ever the case). This incorrect impression can make us miss important aspects of the stories we read. Second, knowing the geographical setting adds depth and richness to the biblical stories. It has been said that not knowing the geographical setting is like watching a play without any scenery.

That setting, for the most part, is the land of Israel, which lies at the east end of the Mediterranean Sea. For much of the Old Testament period, this land was known as Canaan. Canaan was also the name of Noah's grandson. From the fourth century BC on, after the Greeks took over, the land was known as Palestine, from the Greek word for Philistia. This area is the focus of the storyline of the Bible because this is the land God promised to give to his chosen people—the Promised Land.

Israel is part of what is known as the Fertile Crescent, or the Cradle of Civilization. This broad region is the setting of ancient humanity. It is where early, relatively sophisticated societies formed, which developed written language and efficient methods of farming. One of the cities in Israel, Jericho, has been called "the oldest city in the world." It has archaeological finds from 8000–7000 BC.

The land of Israel has been called "the Land Between." That is because it is located between perennial ancient superpowers— Egypt to the southwest, and Syria, Assyria, and Babylon (Iraq) to the north and northeast. (When the setting of the Bible's story is not in Israel itself, it is usually in one of these areas.) When these superpowers would clash, they often had to march through Israel to do it. Also, Israel is located between the Mediterranean Sea to the west and a formidable desert to the east.

This should make us wonder: Why did God give this land to his chosen people? There were certainly better locations on the earth if he really wanted to bless them. So why here?

One possible answer is that he wanted to lovingly test his people. God wants his people anywhere and everywhere to trust him, to depend upon him, and to seek his help. But when things are easy, it is hard for us to do that. It becomes easier for us to trust ourselves and our favorable situations in life. God gave his chosen people a challenging place to live in its in-betweenness. Even within the land there were challenges. Farming was possible, but not easy. Getting around was also a challenge due to the topography of the land. All of this seems to be God's way of encouraging his people to trust him. There is certainly a lesson here for our own challenging situations in life. They are God's way of saying, "Will you trust me to help you through this rather than trusting yourself?"

Not only is the geography of the Bible helpful to know, but so is the topography. The coastal plain along the Mediterranean Sea is flat and good for agriculture. This is where the ancient Philistines lived and where many armies marched through the land. To the east of this plain are low rolling hills and broad valleys. The Hebrew word for this is the *shephelah*, which can be translated "foothills" or "lowlands." It looks like a very peaceful, picturesque area, but many bloody battles took place here in biblical times, such as those between Israel and the Philistines. Farther inland to the east are mountains that reach elevations of 3,000 feet, separated by steep-sided V-shaped valleys. This is called the "hill country" and is the central part of the land where many important events took place. The patriarchs—Abraham, Isaac, and Jacob—lived here, and it is where the new nation of Israel first settled after conquering the land under the leadership of Joshua. It was relatively secure with regard to invading armies, but the mountains and valleys made it a challenging place to live and get around.

To the east of this is the Jordan River Valley, running between the Sea of Galilee to the north and the Dead Sea to the south. This is a geological fault line and very low in elevation. The Dead Sea is the lowest point on earth at 1,300 feet below sea level. There is a very steep decline between the hill country (e.g., the city of Jerusalem) and the Jordan River Valley (e.g., the city of Jericho)—around 4,000 feet over a distance of ten miles or so. The east side of the Jordan River, known as Transjordan, is important too. Two and a half of the twelve tribes of Israel were given permission by God to settle there after the exodus. Some of Israel's historic enemies also lived there, such as the Ammonites and Moabites.

FUN FACT

This tiny little strip of land is *still* the center of the world's attention. That is amazing, especially in light of the fact that the land itself doesn't have much to offer by way of natural resources. But on the other hand, this shouldn't surprise anyone who is familiar with God's work and words in the Bible. This area has a *very* important place in God's big plan, both today, as well as back in Bible times.

How Is the
Old Testament
Organized?

The Old Testament has been organized in different ways down through the centuries. The oldest division seems to be twofold: the Law and the Prophets. The Law refers to the first five books of the Old Testament, also known as the Pentateuch, which is a Greek word meaning "five scrolls" or "five books." These books are Genesis, Exodus, Leviticus, Numbers, and Deuteronomy. The rest of the Old Testament books are considered the Prophets. We could call this way of organizing the books the "biblical division," because the phrase is used repeatedly throughout the Bible.

For example, there may be a hint of this in Israel's confession of sin in Nehemiah 9:29–30: "You warned them in order to turn them back to your *law*. . . . By your Spirit you warned them through your *prophets*." Similar statements can be seen in Daniel's confession of sin in Daniel 9:6 ("prophets"), 11 ("law"), and 13 ("Law of Moses"). The New Testament clearly indicates that this is how the Old Testament was referred to. Jesus said in the Sermon on the Mount: "Do not think that I have come to abolish the Law or the Prophets; I have not come to abolish them but to fulfill them" (Matthew 5:17; see also Matthew 7:12; 22:40). The same designation is used in Acts 13:15: "after the reading from the Law and the Prophets." Paul seemed to have this in mind when he said in one of his defense speeches, "I am saying nothing beyond what the prophets and Moses said would happen" (Acts 26:22).

In another early Jewish tradition, we find a threefold division: The Law (*Torah,* the Hebrew term, which can also mean "instruction" or "teaching"), the Prophets (*Nebi'im*), and the Writings (*Kethubim*), sometimes referred to as *Hagiographa,* a Greek term meaning "holy writings." The earliest reference to this seems to be in the prologue of Ecclesiasticus (around 180 BC): "Not only this book, but even *the Law* itself, *the Prophecies,* and *the rest of the books* differ not a little when read in the original" (italics added). This may also be reflected in Jesus' statement in Luke 24:44: "Everything must be fulfilled that is written about me in the Law of Moses, the Prophets and the Psalms" (the first book in the Writings). This threefold division is still the structure of modern Jewish Scriptures.

In this threefold division, the Law, again, would be the Pentateuch: Genesis, Exodus, Leviticus, Numbers, and Deuteronomy. The Prophets are divided into two subdivisions: the Former Prophets include the books of Joshua, Judges, Samuel, and Kings; the Latter Prophets include the books of Isaiah, Jeremiah, Ezekiel, and the Book of the Twelve (Hosea, Joel, Amos, Obadiah, Jonah, Micah, Nahum, Habakkuk, Zephaniah, Haggai, Zechariah, and Malachi). The third category in the Hebrew canon, the Writings, include Psalms, Proverbs, Job, the Scrolls (*Megillot*)—which include the Song of Solomon, Ruth, Lamentations, Ecclesiastes, and Esther—Daniel, Ezra-Nehemiah, and Chronicles. Organized in this way, the Hebrew Scriptures contain twenty-four books. In some editions, Ruth is attached to the end of Judges, and Lamentations is attached at the end of Jeremiah, resulting in twenty-two books.

The reason why these books are categorized in this way is not clear. For instance, why aren't Daniel and Ezra-Nehemiah in the category of the Prophets like other books that contain historical material? Maybe the best suggestion is that these three categories represent the historical stages in which these various books were recognized as the Word of God.

By at least 100 BC, a fourfold division was introduced in the Septuagint, the Greek translation of the Hebrew Scriptures. The four sections were now Law, History, Poetry, and Prophecy. This is the organization of most modern English translations of the Old Testament. As before, the Law contains the first five books of the Old Testament. The books of History are Joshua, Judges, Ruth, 1 and 2 Samuel, 1 and 2 Kings, 1 and 2 Chronicles, Ezra, Nehemiah, and Esther. The books of Poetry are Job, Psalms, Proverbs, Ecclesiastes, and Song of Solomon. The books of Prophecy are divided into Major and Minor Prophets. This has to do with size only, not importance or significance. The Major Prophets are Isaiah, Jeremiah, Lamentations (due to Jeremiah being the author), Ezekiel, and Daniel. The Minor Prophets are the same as those in the Book of the Twelve mentioned above. This organization results in thirty-nine Old Testament books. These are the same books that are in the threefold division, only divided in different ways.

Even though the order of the Old Testament books has been fixed for quite some time, this has not always been the case. In the threefold Jewish division, the books of the Law always came first and in their present order (Genesis first, Deuteronomy last) due to their importance to the Jewish people and the fact that they were the first books to be written. The order of the Former Prophets has also been the same, reflecting the order of the history they record. But the order of the Latter Prophets has varied historically. Some rabbis preferred to order them from the shortest to the longest. Sometimes the Book of the Twelve was arranged in chronological order of writing, Hosea being the earliest and Malachi being the latest. There is even more variety in how the Writings have been ordered, probably due to the variety of content (history, poetry) and the uncertainty of the dating of some of these books.

The order that we are used to in our modern English Bible reflects the order that was established by the Latin Vulgate, the standard translation of the Bible used in the Middle Ages. This in turn reflects the order of the Septuagint, but even that order has varied in the various editions.

FUN FACT

The Jews have taken the first letters of the Hebrew terms for the categories in the threefold division—*Torah, Nebi'im,* and *Kethubim*—added vowels, and come up with the word *TaNaKh* to refer to their complete Scriptures. They use this word in the same way Christians use the word *Bible.* For example, the Jewish Publication Society's English translation of their Scriptures is entitled *Tanakh: the Holy Scriptures.*

The Biblical Division—Twofold

The Law	The Prophets
Genesis—Deuteronomy	Joshua—Malachi

The Jewish Division—Threefold

The Law Torah	The Prophets Nebi'im	The Writings Kethubim
Genesis Exodus Leviticus Numbers Deuteronomy	**The Former Prophets** Joshua, Judges, Samuel, Kings **The Latter Prophets** Isaiah, Jeremiah, Ezekiel, the Twelve (Minor Prophets)	Psalms, Proverbs, Job, Song of Solomon, Ecclesiastes, Ruth, Lamentations, Daniel, Esther, Ezra-Nehemiah, Chronicles

The Modern Division—Fourfold

Law	History	Poetry	Prophecy
Genesis Exodus Leviticus Numbers Deuteronomy	Joshua, Judges, Ruth, 1 & 2 Samuel, 1 & 2 Kings, 1 & 2 Chronicles, Ezra, Nehemiah, Esther	Job, Psalms, Proverbs, Ecclesiastes, Song of Solomon	**Major:** Isaiah, Jeremiah, Lamentations, Ezekiel, Daniel **Minor:** Hosea, Joel, Amos, Obadiah, Jonah, Micah, Nahum, Habakkuk, Zephaniah, Haggai, Zechariah, Malachi

Who Wrote
the Old Testament?

All of the authors of the books of the Old Testament should be classified as prophets. That term refers to messengers, and that is exactly what these authors were doing—delivering the message of God to the people of God. Some books specifically name the author, other books imply or point to a person as the author, and still other books are anonymous.

One of the most important issues of authorship regards the Pentateuch, the first five books of the Old Testament. The traditional view is that Moses is the author of these books. This has been held by Jews since the Pentateuch was written and by Christians since the first century. Even though the Pentateuch itself does not *directly* state that Moses is the author, there is evidence that indicates this is the case. For example, Moses did receive many of the laws recorded in these books directly from God on Mount Sinai (Exodus 19ff.). Also, several books begin with the statement that

God spoke to Moses and that Moses was to pass the message on to the people of Israel (Leviticus 1:1–2; Numbers 1:1; Deuteronomy 1:1–3). Finally, several times it is said that Moses wrote down what God had told him (Exodus 17:14; 24:4; 34:27).

There is also evidence in other Old Testament books that content in the Pentateuch came through Moses (e.g., Judges 3:4; Ezra 6:18). Most important, Jesus and the authors of the New Testament books also believed that Moses wrote these books (e.g., Luke 24:44; Acts 13:39; 2 Corinthians 3:15–16). These are just a few of the many verses that support the traditional view.

Beginning about 200 years ago, some scholars rejected the traditional view and suggested what has come to be called the Documentary Hypothesis. This theory is that the first five books of the Old Testament were written by a number of different authors living at different times from the ninth century BC (600 years *after* Moses lived) through the fifth century BC (1,000 years *after* Moses lived). Furthermore, the theory claims that yet another group (editors) took bits and pieces of what these authors had written and stitched them together to form what we now know as the Pentateuch. This cut-and-paste theory has been much challenged and sufficiently refuted, but it is still held by some biblical scholars and is often simply assumed in popular books on the Old Testament.

The issue here is important, because the idea that Moses did not write these books calls into question the knowledge and integrity of Jesus Christ as well as the New Testament authors. Fortunately, there is strong evidence that Moses did indeed write these books, and the traditional view can be held with confidence.

All of the Old Testament historical books are anonymous. There are no clear references to authorship. The titles do not *necessarily* reflect the authorship. For example, the death of Samuel is recorded in 1 Samuel 25:1, therefore he could not have written the rest of 1 Samuel or 2 Samuel. Rather, it seems, the titles reflect one of the main characters in the book. It is likely, however, that these main characters may have played a role in the composition of the book in some way. But any conclusion regarding the authorship of these books should be held with a degree of tentativeness, and nothing crucial rests on one's conclusion (unlike the authorship of the Pentateuch).

Authorship of the books of poetry is a mixed bag. The book of Job is anonymous. Suggestions range from Job himself, Elihu (one of the characters in the book), Moses (according to Jewish tradition), and Solomon (because Job is considered wisdom literature and Solomon wrote other wisdom literature).

Some of the psalms have superscriptions that name their authors. According to these, David wrote seventy-three (nearly half of the psalms), Asaph wrote twelve, the sons of Korah wrote twelve, Solomon wrote two, and Moses and Ethan each wrote one. It seems that Asaph, the sons of Korah, and Ethan were Levites who were responsible for leading Israel in worship. It makes sense that they would write psalms, which is the Greek word meaning "songs," for that purpose. The remaining forty-nine psalms are anonymous.

The book of Proverbs names Solomon as its author (1:1; 10:1). Solomon is known as one of the wisest persons to have lived, and the proverbs are evidence of that. The last two chapters of Proverbs, however, are authored by Agur (chap. 30) and Lemuel (chap. 31). Not much is known about these two authors, other than that they seem to be Gentiles who probably lived east of Israel. The book of Ecclesiastes is "the words of the Teacher, son of David, king in Jerusalem" (1:1). Technically, this book is anonymous since no specific name is attached to it. Jewish and Christian tradition is that Solomon is the author; however, some scholars believe that someone later than Solomon wrote it. Since it is anonymous, we should remain tentative regarding its authorship.

Regarding the Song of Solomon, 1:1 could be translated "The Song of Songs, which is Solomon's." Therefore, the traditional

Jewish and Christian view is that Solomon is the author. He is mentioned numerous times as a character in the book. However, 1:1 could also be translated "The Song of Songs, which is for/about Solomon." It is possible, then, that this was written by someone else, probably during Solomon's reign, in order to honor Solomon. Again, the authorship here is ambiguous.

The prophetic books, for the most part, clearly state the author at the very beginning of the book. There are a few exceptions to this general rule. The book of Jonah is technically anonymous. It is also different from most of the other prophetic books in that it is the story of the prophet himself rather than the record of the messages the prophet was given. It may be by Jonah or based on the account as he told it. Lamentations, too, is anonymous. It has traditionally been attributed to Jeremiah, and for that reason it has been placed after the book of Jeremiah and among the prophetic books, even though it is technically a book of poetry.

A few relatively recent challenges regarding prophetic books should be noted, namely the authorship of Isaiah and Daniel. Both of these challenges are due to the amazing predictive prophecy in these books. Some scholars simply assume that no one can predict the future, and even if God can know the future, he doesn't tell anyone what it is. Therefore, they feel compelled to "late date" predictive prophecy. That is, they claim that these "predictions" were written to *appear* as though they were written *before* the events, when in reality they were written afterward—history in the form of prediction. Specifically, some scholars believe that the latter part of Isaiah, chapters 40–66, was written by someone other than Isaiah. A significant problem with this suggestion is that Jesus and other New Testament authors quote from Isaiah frequently, including from chapters 40–66, and attribute the statements to Isaiah (Matthew 4:14–16; John 12:38; Romans 10:16, 20). The same thing has been done to Daniel, due to his amazing vision of the future in chapters 7–12. Some skeptical scholars claim that this was written by someone about 400 years later. However, if we believe that God knows the future because the future is simply the outworking of his plan, there is no problem in believing that these prophets made these amazingly accurate predictions.

FUN FACT

Some of the prophets' names were significant. Isaiah means "the salvation of God." This is the main theme of his book; he uses the word twenty-six times, compared to seven in all of the other prophets combined. Zephaniah means "God hides" in order to protect. The latter part of Zephaniah 2:3 says, "Seek righteousness, seek humility; perhaps you will be sheltered on the day of the LORD's anger." The name Malachi seems most appropriate for a prophet of God; it means "my messenger."

For Whom Was the
Old Testament Written?

Because the Old Testament is the inspired Word of God, in the broadest sense these books were written for every one of us. That is why God made these books available to us thousands of years after they were written. But from the human authors' point of view, these books were written to a specific audience—their own contemporaries—and for a specific purpose: to meet a need at that time. In this sense, the original audience for the books of the Old Testament was the nation of Israel, God's chosen people.

The earliest books of the Old Testament, Genesis through Deuteronomy, were written by Moses for the brand-new nation of Israel in the forty years following the exodus. One reason Moses wrote them is because Israel needed to know their God who had just delivered them from enslavement and declared himself to be the King of this new nation. They needed to know that he was the creator of all things, thus Genesis 1–2. They needed to know that he had entered into a covenant relationship with their forefather

Abraham and that this covenant was passed on to his descendants—Isaac, Jacob, and his twelve sons, thus Genesis 12–50. They also needed to know what he, as their King, expected of them, thus the many laws in Exodus, Leviticus, and Deuteronomy. It was also important for them to know that even though all the people around them—the people of Egypt, where they had come from, and the people of Canaan, where they were going—believed in many gods, Israel's God and King was the one and only true God. Thus, the plagues described in Exodus 9 showed the gods of Egypt not to be real gods (Exodus 9:27), and the Israelites were commanded not to worship any other gods (Exodus 20:2–3).

Another reason Moses wrote these books was because the new nation of Israel needed to know their relationship to the one true God. They were in an eternal covenant with God because they were the descendants of Abraham, Isaac, and Jacob. And because God was a holy God, they were to be holy people; they were to reflect God's nature. This included being loyal to him in their covenant relationship with him and in obeying the laws he had given them.

The books of history were also written for the nation of Israel, but centuries later than the books of Moses, and with the specific purpose of demonstrating historically that God meant what he said in the Law: He would bless them for their obedience and curse them for their disobedience. Tragically, these books also chronicle the perpetual slide of God's people into increasing sinfulness, and therefore provided the reason for Israel's eventual exile from the land God had given to them. This was exactly what God had said he would do.

The books of poetry were originally written to Israel as well. Their purpose was to teach them to be wise and provide means by which they could appropriately pray to, and worship, God. In fact, most of the psalms have an audience in addition to humans, and that is God himself. They were initially inspired by God for Israel, but more specifically they were to be used by Israel to communicate with God in the right way through prayer and worship. These are God-given models for all of God's people. They help us to be open and honest with God as we speak to him and express our genuine thoughts, emotions, and attitudes. Thus we have psalms that help us express our joy, happiness, thankfulness to, and adoration of, God. We also have psalms that help us express our frustration, loneliness, despair, anger (even toward God).

The prophetic books, too, were initially written for the nation of Israel, but at a time when they were particularly sinful and wandering further and further away from God. The specific purpose of these books was to confront Israel with their sinfulness and to call them to repentance, faithfulness to God, and obedience to God. The alternative would be to experience the judgment of God.

Sometimes, the prophets' message might imply that the audience was a specific Gentile nation or the Gentile nations in general, but even then the message was really intended for God's people, the Israelites. For example, there are two prophetic books that had to do with God's intention to judge the city of Nineveh (the Assyrians). The book of Jonah is about the prophet Jonah, whom God directed to go to Nineveh to announce impending divine judgment. Jonah didn't want to do this because he feared they would repent and then experience God's forgiveness rather than his wrath. So he tried to escape the responsibility, but God chased him down and gave him a second chance. Jonah did obey the second time, but with resentment, and the Ninevites did indeed repent just as he had feared (Jonah 4:2). The main point of this book, however, is not the sin of Nineveh or the repentance of Nineveh, nor is it about futile attempts to run away from God. Rather, the point is to confront the attitude of God's people in Judah toward non-Jews, as illustrated by Jonah himself. They had come to believe that God was only for the Jews and that he wanted to bless only them, and that anybody else (people they referred to as Gentiles), especially those as cruel and arrogant as the Assyrians, only deserved God's judgment. They had forgotten that God wanted to bless *all* nations through them (Genesis 12:3). God's message for Israel in the book of Jonah, then, was to love and care about all people, just as God does.

About a century later, the Ninevites had returned to their sinful ways, and God again intended to judge them. That is the main theme of the book of Nahum (1:1, 8–11). But again, the intended audience was not Nineveh, but God's chosen people, Israel. The purpose was to bring them comfort by knowing that God would judge the Ninevites because of their cruelty and abuse of God's people. In fact, the prophet's name, *Nahum,* means "comfort." That comfort can be heard in 1:15: "Look, there on the mountains, the feet of one who brings good news [the Assyrians have fallen], who proclaims peace [because the Assyrians are no longer a threat]! Celebrate your festivals, Judah, and fulfill your vows. No more will the wicked invade you; they will be completely destroyed" (compare 3:19). The point is that you shouldn't mess with God's people, and that God wants his people to know that he will right the wrongs that have been committed against them.

The Old Testament books were originally written for God's Old Testament covenant people, Israel, at various times in history and for various reasons. But in God's broader perspective, these books contain important truths and great lessons for all people of all time.

FUN FACT?

I don't know this to be a fact, but I suspect that the authors of the books of the Old Testament would never have dreamed that people around the world would be continuing to read what they wrote, even thousands of years later. God knew this, but I think the writers would have been absolutely amazed by it.

9

What Will I Find
in the Pentateuch?

The books of the Bible can be placed in different categories of literature called *genres*. The main genres of the Old Testament are history, poetry, and prophecy. We'll take a look at these over the next four chapters.

The first five books of the Old Testament fit within the genre of history, and because they are so important, we will devote an entire chapter to them. As mentioned in earlier chapters, these books are known by various names: the Pentateuch, which is Greek for "five books"; the Torah, which is Hebrew for "instruction" or "law"; the books of Moses, since he is the author; and the Law, because they contain God's law for his people, Israel. This latter term is how Jesus and the New Testament authors referred to these books (e.g., Matthew 5:17; Acts 13:15).

Moses wrote these books after the exodus from Egypt and the establishment of God's chosen people as a nation. They are the foundational documents of this new nation and contain what God's people needed to know to live before their King, God himself, and to live together as a society that reflects the nature of their King.

The book of Genesis is sometimes called "The Book of Beginnings" because it is the first book of the Bible and records important beginnings in God's plan. First, it tells us of the beginning of the universe, which God as Creator brought into existence from nothing (1:1). Second, it tells us about the beginning of humanity, when God created man and woman in his image (1:27). Third, it tells us about the beginning of the divine institution of marriage (2:22–24). Fourth, it tells us about the origin of sin (3:1–7), the consequences of sin (3:16–19), God's judgment of sin (3:22–24), and also, the remedy for sin: namely, sacrifice (possibly implied in 3:21, but certainly made clear later on). Fifth, Genesis tells us of the beginning of the family, when Adam and Eve began to have children (4:1–2). Sixth, it tells us of the beginning of occupations (4:20–24, where you will find references to agriculture, industry, and the arts). Seventh, it tells us of the beginning of ethnic groups or nations (chapters 10 and 11). Finally, Genesis tells us of the beginning of the "chosen" nation (chapter 12).

This last beginning is significant because, in the first eleven chapters of Genesis, God had been dealing with humanity as a whole, whereas from chapter 12 on, he narrows his focus to one man, Abraham (originally known as Abram). From there, God begins to carry out his plan through this man and his descendants, who were known at this point as "the Hebrews" (e.g., Genesis 14:13). The rest of the book of Genesis records the lives of the early generations of God's chosen people, known as "the patriarchs"—Abraham, Isaac, Jacob, and Jacob's twelve sons. Genesis 12–50 is the story of the patriarchs' faith (often imperfect and weak) in the promises that God had given them and how God began to fulfill those promises.

The book of Exodus continues the story in Egypt. God had told Jacob to move his family to Egypt (Genesis 46:3) where he had providentially established Jacob's son, Joseph, as second in command over Egypt in order to provide a place for the family of Jacob to grow. God blessed them so greatly that their population exploded, which threatened the native Egyptians. This resulted in the Egyptians oppressing and enslaving the Hebrews, which God, long before, told Abraham would happen (Genesis 15:13–14). The Hebrews called out to God for deliverance, God heard their prayers, and he chose one of their own, Moses, to be their deliverer. The exodus is the great event through which God, through Moses, delivered his people from their enslavement, led them out of Egypt into the wilderness, and established them as the nation of Israel with himself as their King.

It was at this point that God gave his people the constitution of their new nation—the law. This included the Ten Commandments, but also some six hundred plus additional, more specific laws. The whole body of the law is found in the latter part of Exodus (chapters 20ff.), essentially all of Leviticus, parts of Numbers, and most of Deuteronomy. It is this material that gave the title (the Law) to all five books of Moses.

These hundreds of laws can be summarized in three categories: The moral category includes general principles, such as the Ten Commandments, that helped God's people live before him in a way that pleased him. The rest of these laws work these principles out in greater detail. The civil category includes those laws that helped God's people live together as a society. Within this category are criminal law, family law, business law, social welfare law, among others. The ceremonial category includes laws regarding how to worship God through religious ceremonies or rituals. For example, there were laws applying to the place of worship (the tabernacle), the priests, sacrifices, holy days, and feasts.

After about thirteen months in the wilderness, the new nation was ready to go back to Canaan—the land that God had promised would be theirs forever. The book of Numbers records this journey, which includes twelve spies being sent to report on the land, the nation's unwillingness to trust God to help them conquer the land, and God's judgment of forty years' wandering in the wilderness. The purpose of this long wait was to eliminate the unbelieving generation of Israel. They did not trust God, and therefore forfeited the privilege of experiencing God's promises. Instead, they died in the wilderness. At the end of this period, God led his people around the east side of the Dead Sea and put them just across the Jordan River from Canaan.

This is the setting of the last book of the Pentateuch. The name of the book summarizes the contents. *Deuteronomy* means "second law," because Moses, shortly before his death, repeated the law of God to the second generation of Israel. It was now their responsibility to keep the law when God brought them into the land of Canaan. How that happened is recorded in the first of the historical books—Joshua.

FUN FACT

The Sadducees, a Jewish sect in Jesus' day, accepted *only* these five books of the Old Testament as the authoritative Word of God; they rejected the rest of the Old Testament.

What Will I Find in the Historical Books?

The historical books of the Old Testament are Joshua, Judges, Ruth, 1 and 2 Samuel, 1 and 2 Kings, and 1 and 2 Chronicles. All of these, except 1 and 2 Chronicles, were classified by the Jews as Former Prophets. Today we often think of prophets as those who predict the future, but the Bible uses the term to mean any messenger of God. These books were therefore regarded as God's message delivered to God's people by prophets. *Former* in this sense doesn't mean that they *used to be* prophets, but that these prophetic books come before the major and minor prophets, which we'll talk about in a later chapter. The Former Prophets are also called by scholars Deuteronomic History, because they contain history that is told from a prophetic perspective through the lens of God's law as recorded in the book of Deuteronomy. That is, these historians recorded how when Israel obeyed God, he blessed them, and when they disobeyed God, he cursed them—just as he said he would in Deuteronomy. Their concern in this history is morality, first and foremost.

There are some similarities between Old Testament history and other ancient Near Eastern sacred texts (e.g., from Babylonia, the *Atrakhasis Epic* and the *Gilgamesh Epic*). But in contrast to other ancient texts, which were full of mythology—stories of what the gods were supposedly doing up in the heavens—the Old Testament historical books recorded true history—what God was actually doing down on earth. Also, there are many similarities between Old Testament history writing and modern history writing, such as a desire to be accurate and record events truthfully. But in contrast to modern history writing, which strives to be objective, Old Testament history writing (along with all ancient history writing) was intended to be persuasive. Ancient historians were not content to write history just for the sake of recording events; they wanted to persuade their audience to think and behave in a certain way. There was always a "moral" to the stories they were recording— something to be learned. That does not mean they twisted the facts in order to convince their readers of something. They cared about accuracy—after all, these events were about God, who is the standard of morality and truthfulness. But they were more concerned that their readers become godlier rather than merely more knowledgeable.

The book of Joshua is the story of Israel's invasion of Canaan, the Promised Land. It covers about ten years after the forty years in the wilderness. It includes the famous story of the battle of Jericho, along with a record of other battles with the Canaanites. In all of these, God gave his people great victories. The latter part of the book describes how the conquered land was divided between the twelve tribes of Israel. Joshua 21:43–45 provides a good summary: "So the LORD gave Israel all the land he had sworn to give their ancestors, and they took possession of it and settled there. The LORD gave them rest on every side, just as he had sworn to their ancestors. Not one of their enemies withstood them; the LORD gave all their enemies into their hands. Not one of all the

LORD's good promises to the house of Israel failed; every one was fulfilled." So the book of Joshua records the faithfulness of God to keep his promises, but also the faith God's people had in God to fulfill those promises. Both parts are important.

The book of Judges is quite a contrast to the book of Joshua. During this period, the people of Israel failed to honor God with their trust and obedience. This is primarily because they did not do what God had clearly and repeatedly told them to do: Completely expel the Canaanites (e.g., Deuteronomy 7:1–5; 20:16–18). Several times the opening chapter repeats that "they did not drive [the Canaanites] out" (Judges 1:21, 27, 29–33). As a result, the Israelites were entangled in two sins: intermarriage with the Canaanites and the practice of Canaanite worship, otherwise known as idolatry (Judges 3:6). Most of the book conveys a repeating six-stage cycle. First, the Israelites sin (3:7). Second, God punishes his people by allowing their enemies to invade the land and oppress them (e.g., 3:8). Third, God's people eventually repent and cry to God for deliverance (3:9). Fourth, God provides deliverance through a judge, who was usually a military leader. Fifth, the judge defeats the invaders and drives them out of the land (3:9–10). Finally, things go well until the cycle repeats itself (3:11). The last verse of the book says it all: "In those days Israel had no king; everyone did as he saw fit" (21:25).

The story of Ruth is set during this same terribly sinful period in Israel's history, but there is a stark contrast between the two books. Ruth illustrates that even in the darkest periods of sin God preserves those who are faithful to him. Also in this book we find important family background regarding the line of the promised Messiah.

First and Second Samuel record the transition from the period of the judges to the monarchy of Israel. Samuel was the last judge, but now God's people wanted a human king. This was a sinful desire, but God knew they would want this and intended to provide a human king for them all along. God appointed Saul as the first king of Israel. Unfortunately, he failed to obey God, and God removed the throne from him and gave it to "a man after [God's] own heart"—David (1 Samuel 13:14). God blessed the reign of David (2 Samuel 5:10), and David became the greatest king in Israel's history. But he was also a great sinner (2 Samuel 11), whom God forgave in response to David's confession (2 Samuel 12:13).

First and Second Kings continues the story with David's successor, his son Solomon. But due to Solomon's sin, God divided the kingdom of Israel after Solomon's death. The northern kingdom of Israel was ruled by nineteen kings, from nine royal families, over a period of about two centuries. The author of these books assesses all of them as bad kings, since they all promoted idolatry. The southern kingdom of Judah was ruled by nineteen kings and one queen, all from the Davidic royal family (except the queen), over about three and a half centuries. Some of these kings were assessed as good (e.g., Hezekiah and Josiah), but many of them were bad to very bad, because they also promoted terrible idolatrous practices. But in the end, God did what he had told them he would do in response to ongoing disobedience: he threw his people out of their land. In 722 BC, the kingdom of Israel fell to the Assyrians and was taken into exile. In 586 BC, the kingdom of Judah fell to the Babylonians and was taken into exile.

First and Second Chronicles repeat much of the history found in the books of Samuel and Kings, but from a priestly perspective rather than a prophetic one. In other words, Chronicles emphasizes spiritual matters, such as the worship of God, more than moral matters, or obedience to God. The history here is also presented more positively than the history in Samuel and Kings. The focus is more on God's faithfulness than Israel's unfaithfulness.

The final books of history—Ezra, Nehemiah, and Esther—record the end of Old Testament history after God allowed his people to return from their exile. We are told here of the rebuilding of the temple that had been destroyed in 586 BC, the rebuilding of the walls of Jerusalem, the rebuilding of God's people spiritually through the ministry of Ezra and various prophets, and the reestablishment of God's people in the Promised Land. The main point of these three books is that God is faithful to his covenant promises. He preserved his people from an attempted genocide (the story of Esther), and he brought them back to the land he had promised them (the stories of Ezra and Nehemiah).

FUN FACT

This may not be fun, but it is certainly fitting to note: The history of Israel is characterized by persistent sinfulness, broken occasionally by brief revivals. It should leave the reader wondering: *What is the solution to all of this sinfulness?* That question is answered in the New Testament.

What Will I Find in the Wisdom and Poetry Books?

The second main genre in the Old Testament is poetry. This includes the books of Job, Psalms, Proverbs, Ecclesiastes, and Song of Solomon (although poetry can be found in other books, such as Genesis 49, 2 Samuel 22, and most of the books of prophecy). Whereas prose, as is used in the historical books, is more of a direct form of communication, poetry is more indirect. Rather than primarily feeding the intellect as prose does, poetry also appeals to the reader's emotions and imagination.

Poetry may be better described than defined, so let's look at some of the main characteristics of Hebrew poetry. The most important feature is called parallelism, and has to do with the relationship or correspondence between two or more lines of poetry. The most frequent form is synonymous parallelism, where the second line repeats the thought of the first but uses different words, or synonyms. For example, Psalm 19:1 says, "The heavens declare the glory of God; the skies proclaim the work of his hands." Antithetic parallelism is where the second line contains antonyms or words with the opposite meaning. This form develops a contrast and is used a lot in the book of Proverbs: "A wise son brings joy to his father, but a foolish son brings grief to his mother" (10:1). Chiastic parallelism is also used frequently. Here the second line reverses the order of the first line. Psalm 1:2 says, "But his delight is in the law of the LORD, and in His law he meditates day and night" (NASB). Understanding and recognizing parallelism is not usually important when it comes to interpreting the poem correctly but it is important in order to appreciate the artistry of the poet.

Another characteristic of Hebrew poetry and something that is absolutely crucial with regard to correct interpretation of poetry in general is imagery. Often the imagery in the Bible works with the reader's imagination by comparing a familiar aspect of life to a moral or spiritual truth. Biblical imagery can be challenging because the original audience of this ancient literature was familiar with things that modern readers may not be (e.g., agriculture or animals). The most common forms of imagery are similes and metaphors. A simile is an explicit comparison, using the words *like* or *as*. In Psalm 42:1, we have "As the deer pants for streams of water, so my soul pants for you, my God." A metaphor is an implicit or direct comparison in which one thing is directly identified with another: "The LORD is my shepherd" (Psalm 23:1), not the LORD is *like* my shepherd.

Hebrew poetry also uses many figures of speech. For example, hyperbole is the use of exaggeration to make a point. David said, "I am worn out from my groaning. All night long I flood my bed with weeping and drench my couch with tears" (Psalm 6:6). Did he really flood his bed? Of course not. He was simply making a point about how much he was overcome with grief. Another figure of speech, anthropomorphism, describes God as having human body parts. References to the eyes, ears, hand, and arm of God are common in the Psalms. Similarly, personification is a description of inanimate objects in terms of human characteristics. Psalm 96:11 says, "Let the heavens rejoice, let the earth be glad."

Moving on from the characteristics of Hebrew poetry, let's take a look at the individual wisdom and poetry books. The book of Job addresses the important issue of suffering. Why do the righteous suffer? What is the purpose of suffering? It addresses these questions by telling the story of Job, a righteous and wealthy man whom God allows to experience deep personal pain and loss. But why? Chapters 3–37 record a poetic discussion between Job and four of his friends about this very question. They try to convince him that he is suffering because of his sin. He rejects that idea, but still can't understand the reason for his suffering. Chapters 38–42 contain a rapid-fire succession of rhetorical questions (another figure of speech) that God asks Job. The point of these questions seems to be to put Job in his place. Job isn't God; God is God. Interestingly, the book ends without Job ever understanding the purpose behind his suffering. The point? We are to trust God whether we understand what he is doing or not.

The book of Psalms is made up of 150 poems. The word *psalm* means "song" and many of the poems were put to music. This relates to their purpose: to provide a means through which God's people can communicate with him through worship and prayer. These psalms are primarily directed Godward. God himself is the intended audience.

It might be helpful to know that there are different categories of psalms. Knowing how the psalms fit into these categories will help you use them in the right way. Praise psalms are easy to recognize because they contain exuberant praise for God, and they are very upbeat and positive (e.g., Psalm 113). Use these when you are brimming over with admiration and thanksgiving for God. At the other end of the scale are the lament psalms. These are moody and filled with complaints about the psalmist himself, his enemies, and even God (e.g., Psalms 6 and 69). Use these when you are upset with life and just need to be honest with God about that. Another category is penitential psalms, or psalms of confession. These are used to express sorrow for sin and to request forgiveness from God (e.g., Psalms 38 and 51). Use these when you feel overwhelmed with your own sinfulness.

The book of Proverbs is intended to teach wisdom in life based upon reverence for God (1:2–7; 9:10). A proverb is simply a wise saying or moral principle. Wisdom refers to the ability to live skillfully, that is, the ability to practically apply knowledge to life.

The book of Ecclesiastes is a challenge because it seems so pessimistic. Although it primarily comes across as negative, it teaches something very positive: true happiness can *only* be found in *God*. The book records the search for true meaning, happiness, satisfaction, and fulfillment in things other than God. The result of that search is frustration—"Everything is meaningless!" (1:2; 12:8). Everything, that is, except God and what he provides.

The Song of Solomon is a love story at its best. It illustrates through beautiful poetic expressions the love between a man and a woman, a husband and a wife, as God always intended it to be.

FUN FACT

There are more lament psalms than any other type of psalm! Could that be because God knows we need a lot of help honestly communicating negative thoughts and emotions to him, especially when they are about him?

What Will I Find
in the Prophets?

The primary role of the prophet was to represent God before the people of God by proclaiming the message of God. The main Hebrew word translated *prophet* literally means "speaker" or "messenger." We have already seen that the authors of the Old Testament historical books were considered prophets since that history was also God's message for his people. Moses was also a prophet (Deuteronomy 34:10). The books we are considering now, however, were written later in Old Testament history, from about the eighth century to the fifth century BC, when God's people, Israel, were spiraling further and further away from him into sin. God's gracious response was to send more and more prophets as his messengers to address that dangerous situation.

The Old Testament books of prophecy are grouped into two categories: Major Prophets and Minor Prophets. This has to do with size alone, not significance. The Major Prophets are Isaiah, Jeremiah, Lamentations (technically a poetic book, but placed here due to Jeremiah being its author), Ezekiel, and Daniel. The Minor Prophets are Hosea, Joel, Amos, Obadiah, Jonah, Micah, Nahum, Habakkuk, Zephaniah, Haggai, Zechariah, and Malachi.

Even though the terms *prophet* or *prophecy* tend to make us think about predictions regarding the future, this was actually a minor part of their message. The whole of the prophets' message is sometimes categorized as forth-telling or proclamation prophecy. They told forth or proclaimed God's message. More often than not, this was about things that were happening in the present, not the future. Within that category is a much smaller sub-category that is sometimes called foretelling, or predictive prophecy. It, too, was proclaiming God's message, but now specifically regarding what God intended to do in the future.

The books of prophecy are a big chunk of the Old Testament and contain a lot of details. It is easy to get overwhelmed and a bit lost along the way, so it may help to keep in mind four broad themes into which nearly all of what the prophets had to say would fit. The first theme is *confrontation of sin*. Sometimes this was in broad and general terms: "You are a rebellious and wicked people." Sometimes it was more specific: "You are guilty of idolatry, injustice, and greed." An example would be Isaiah 1:4.

The second theme is a *call for repentance*. This was implied in the confrontation so sometimes was not even stated, but expected to be understood. Other times it was explicit (see, for example, Ezekiel 14:6 and 18:30). These two themes had to do with what was presently going on among God's people.

The third theme is *warning of judgment*. If the people refused to repent of their sin, God would judge them sooner or later, as he had told them he would all the way back in the Mosaic law (e.g., Deuteronomy 28:15–68). Ultimately this judgment would take the form of evicting them from the Promised Land (e.g., Deuteronomy 28:41, 63–65). In most prophetic books, there are also warnings of divine judgment against Gentile nations (e.g., Isaiah

13–23; Jeremiah 46–51; Ezekiel 25–32). This was due to their own sinfulness, such as idolatry (e.g., Jeremiah 48:7, 13, 46—Chemosh was the primary god of Moab; 50:2) and pride (e.g., Isaiah 16:6; Jeremiah 50:31–32; Obadiah 3), but also due to their mistreatment of God's chosen people, Israel (e.g., Isaiah 25:12–14; Obadiah 10). The point is, you don't mess with God's people; God will make things right! God wants his people to know that and be comforted ("Nahum" means comfort, and that is the purpose of the book by that title). This theme has to do with the very near future so it is considered predictive prophecy.

The fourth and final theme is *assurance of hope*. Whereas the first three themes are negative, dark, and heavy, this one is positive and upbeat. Furthermore, because the vast majority of the prophets' messages were made up of the first three themes, especially sin and judgment, this fourth theme is like a breath of fresh air! It is a vital part of God's message, though, because God is faithful to his *unconditional* covenant promises—promises that had nothing to do with his people's faithfulness or obedience. Two of those unconditional promises were that Israel would always be his people and that the land would always be their possession. So even if God had to deal with their sinfulness and lack of repentance, there was always hope on the other side. He would restore them as his people and return them to their land (e.g., Deuteronomy 30:1–5). One important aspect of this assurance of hope was messianic prophecy. Ultimately, the hope of God's people was in the anointed one—the Messiah—who would be sent by God to once and for all completely fulfill God's covenant promises to them. This, of course, anticipated Jesus Christ. One of the best examples here is Isaiah 53. Parts of this chapter are so specific they sound like they came right out of the New Testament: "But he was pierced for our transgressions, he was crushed for our iniquities; the punishment that brought us peace was upon him, and by his wounds we are healed. . . . My righteous servant will justify the many, and he will bear their iniquities" (vv. 5, 11). This theme is purely predictive prophecy, announcing what God would indeed do in the future, including both the first and second comings of Jesus Christ.

Since the ultimate judgment of God happened when the Israelites were thrown out of the Land into exile, the books of prophecy are often classified according to that event. Most of them are preexilic. These are the ones that warned that God's judgment was looming. In general chronological order, they are Joel (although the dating of this book is difficult), Jonah, Amos, Hosea, Isaiah, Micah, Nahum, Zephaniah, Habakkuk, Jeremiah, and Obadiah (this book is also hard to date). The exilic books are Daniel and Ezekiel. The entire prophetic ministry of these two men took place in the Babylonian exile. The postexilic books of prophecy are Haggai, Zechariah, and Malachi. These prophets ministered at the end of Old Testament history after God had brought many of his people back to the land from exile, as he promised he would.

FUN FACT

Ezekiel was a very skilled and creative communicator. Not only was he a preacher and poet, as were most of the prophets, he was also an actor (e.g., 4:1-8; 12:1-16), storyteller (e.g., 15:1-8; 24:1-14), and seer of visions (e.g., chapters 1-3).

What Happened
Between the Old and
New Testaments?

The book of Daniel contains some amazing visions that were given to Daniel. In those visions, God showed him what would happen in the future as he worked out his perfect plan for history and humanity. Parts of these visions cover the latter part of Old Testament history, while other parts seem to refer to the future even from our perspective. But there are also visions that cover what would happen between the close of the Old Testament period and the opening of the New Testament period. This era has been called the 400 silent years, because God did not communicate to his people between the writing of the book of Malachi and the angelic messenger sent to tell Zechariah that he and his wife would have the baby we know as John the Baptist (Luke 1:11–20). This period is also called the intertestamental period. During this time, God was at work setting the stage for the most important event in human history—the physical entrance of God himself into the world in the person of his Son, Jesus Christ.

In chapter 7, Daniel records a vision of four beasts. An angel tells Daniel that these four beasts stand for four kings or kingdoms that would arise (7:16–17). The information in the vision was the same as that revealed through King Nebuchadnezzar's dream in chapter 2. Both the golden head of the statue in the dream and the lion in Daniel's vision stand for the Babylonian Empire of Daniel's own day (2:37–38). The chest and arms of silver in Nebuchadnezzar's dream, and the bear in Daniel's vision, stand for the next kingdom: the Medo-Persian Empire (2:39). The Persians defeated the Babylonians in 539 BC, also during Daniel's time. The belly and thighs of bronze in chapter 2, and the leopard in chapter 7, stand for the Greek Empire, which was established when Alexander the Great defeated the Persians in 333 BC. This took place in the intertestamental period. The last part of the statue in Nebuchadnezzar's dream was the legs of iron and feet of iron and clay. The fourth beast of Daniel's vision was "terrifying and frightening and very powerful" (7:7). These seem to refer to the Roman Empire, which displaced the Greek Empire in 63 BC. This empire was the world superpower when the New Testament period began.

Daniel's last vision, recorded in chapters 10–12, was a full and detailed prediction of much of what would happen between the Old and New Testament periods. Alexander the Great died at age thirty-two, and his empire was divided among four of his generals (11:3–4). Two of those, and their resulting kingdoms, are important from the perspective of the land of Palestine. General Ptolemy was given Egypt and Palestine, and he and his descendants are referred to in the book of Daniel as the "king of the South" (e.g., 11:5, 9ff.). General Seleucus was given the area to the north of Palestine (Syria, Babylon, and Asia Minor). He and his descendants are referred to as the "king of the North" (11:6–8ff.). Rule over Palestine shifted from the south to the north when Antiochus the Great, a Seleucid king, took it away from the Ptolemaic king in 198 BC (11:15–16).

Eventually, one of Antiochus's sons, known as Antiochus IV Epiphanes, succeeded him in 175 BC (11:21). This king is one of the great villains of Jewish history due to his violent repression of the Jews under his rule (11:28–32). As a part of this repression, he appointed a Jewish high priest who would be loyal to himself. He outlawed the Jewish sacrifices, feasts, Sabbath observance, ritual of circumcision, and reading of their Scriptures. He forced many Jews to offer sacrifices to his primary god, Zeus. Worst of all, in December of 167 BC, he set up an altar to Zeus in the temple of God in Jerusalem, and on that altar, he sacrificed a pig—an unclean animal according to the Mosaic Law! This is referred to in Daniel 11:31 as "the abomination that causes desolation."

All of this prompted an uprising on the part of the Jews (11:33–35) known as the Maccabean revolt, after one of its leaders, Judas Maccabeus. Judas and his brothers were great military leaders, and the revolt was very successful. In December, 164 BC, the temple, which had been recaptured, was cleansed and rededicated to the worship of God. Hanukkah is the annual Jewish holiday that commemorates this important event. It is referred to as the Festival of Dedication in John 10:22. The fight for independence continued until the Jews gained political freedom in 143 BC. This is noteworthy because they had been under Gentile domination since the initial Babylonian invasion of Judah in 605 BC—over 400 years!

Two important Jewish sects in the first century AD, the Pharisees and the Sadducees, find their roots in this period of history. The Pharisees came from the *Hasidim*, or "loyal ones." These were the Jews who resisted Antiochus's repressions and remained loyal to their Jewish convictions. The Sadducees came from the Jews who were more willing to compromise their Jewish conviction in order to get along with Antiochus. Both of these groups are mentioned frequently in the Gospels.

The Jewish rule of Palestine known as the Maccabean Period is usually dated from 164 BC. There was a series of kings who were priests but not legitimate Davidic kings. At the end of this period, two brothers fought for control and the Romans took advantage of the instability. They marched in and took over in 63 BC, ending the relatively brief period of Jewish freedom and control over Palestine—100 years. This set the stage for the political situation into which the Son of God was born and lived his earthly life.

God's providential work can be seen in this intertestamental period through the three main ethnic groups at that time. The Greeks provided a universal language, which many people used in the first century. The Old Testament had been translated into Greek by this time, and the New Testament was written in Greek. The Romans provided what is called the Peace of Rome, or *Pax Romana*. Due to their military might, things were relatively stable and peaceful. The Romans also built highways throughout their empire. This provided a good environment for the spread of the gospel. The Jewish influence came through what is known as the Jewish Dispersion, or *Diaspora,* referring to the fact that Jews lived throughout the Roman Empire. As a result, there was a general understanding among Gentiles of the concepts of monotheism—that there is only one true God, and the Jewish messianic expectation—that God would send the "anointed one" to reestablish the Jewish kingdom and Davidic reign. These concepts were a necessary foundation for understanding the gospel of Jesus Christ. The Jews had also established synagogues throughout the empire. These became the prototypes for Christian local churches, where new believers in Christ were gathered to be taught and encouraged. All of this demonstrates God's amazing, sovereign work in the years between the Old and New Testament periods. He was setting the stage for the coming of his Son to accomplish the great work of salvation through his sinless life, sacrificial death, and victorious resurrection.

FUN FACT

We haven't considered the most important part of Nebuchadnezzar's dream and Daniel's visions: God's kingdom *will* eventually replace all human kingdoms. It will last *forever* (Daniel 2:44–45; 7:13–14, 18, 27), and his people will enjoy it forever. "Everyone whose name is found written in the book [the righteous]—will be delivered . . . [they] will awake . . . to everlasting life [the resurrection] . . . [and they] will shine like the brightness of the heavens, and those who lead many to righteousness, like the stars for ever and ever" (Daniel 12:1–3).

How Is the New Testament Organized?

Like the Old Testament, the New Testament is organized by genres, or types of literature. There are four: the Gospels, history, the Epistles, and prophecy.

The Gospels—Matthew, Mark, Luke, and John—come first because they introduce us to Jesus Christ, the focus of the New Testament (and the anticipation of the Old Testament). In these books we are told of the birth, life, ministry, death, and resurrection of the Son of God. Although these books recount true events, just as the history books do, they are not generally put in that genre since the events are so selective (more on this in chapter 17). We call this genre *gospel,* meaning "good news," because Jesus is the pivot point of the Bible, and what he did is the happy ending to the entire story of Scripture. It makes sense that the books that record this would come first in the New Testament—after all, this is very important information.

The category of history has only one book—Acts. This book carries on from where the Gospels ended: Jesus entrusted the task of spreading the good news of what he had accomplished to his followers. They were eventually to take it to "the ends of the earth" (Acts 1:8). This book also acts as a transition between the Gospels and the next category, the Epistles. As we will see, the book of Acts provides us with the historical setting of quite a few of the Epistles.

The third category, the Epistles, contains twenty-one letters (*epistle* is another word for "letter") to churches or individuals. This can be broken down into two sub-categories. The Pauline Epistles are the thirteen letters written by the apostle Paul. Our Bible organizes them by length (largest to smallest) and audience (church or individual) as follows: Romans, 1 Corinthians, 2 Corinthians, Galatians, Ephesians, Philippians, Colossians, 1 Thessalonians, 2 Thessalonians, 1 Timothy, 2 Timothy, Titus, and Philemon. The second sub-category is the General Epistles, sometimes referred to as the Catholic Epistles, the word *catholic* meaning "general" or "universal." These were written by authors other than Paul and were written to more general audiences (for the most part) rather than specific churches or individuals, as Paul's letters were. Their order in our Bible is as follows: Hebrews, James, 1 Peter, 2 Peter, 1 John, 2 John, 3 John, and Jude. These books are ordered by length (Hebrews is the longest; Jude is one of the shortest) and by author (Peter's two letters and John's three letters are grouped together).

The final main category of the New Testament is prophecy. It contains only one book—Revelation. Most of this book anticipates the future, when God will wrap up his plan for creation once and for all by removing sin and its effects and restoring the universe to the state in which he created it. These great events revolve around the second coming of his Son, Jesus Christ, to judge all people and then rule on the earth.

A drawback of the organization of the New Testament, especially the Epistles, is that they are not grouped in chronological order. However, the historical setting of these letters is often helpful in better understanding their content. So what follows is a brief explanation of the chronological order of these letters.

Most of Paul's letters fit in the flow of the latter part of the book of Acts. His earliest letter, Galatians, was written after his first missionary journey, when he and Barnabas established four new churches in the province of Galatia. It would probably fit between Acts 14 and 15. First and Second Thessalonians were written during Paul's second missionary journey. He was at Corinth, but he wrote these letters to the new Christians in the church that he had founded in Thessalonica. These letters would fit somewhere in Acts 18:1–17. During his third missionary journey, Paul wrote three more letters. He was in Ephesus when he wrote his first letter to the new church in Corinth, just across the Aegean Sea. This would fit somewhere in Acts 19. He wrote to the Corinthians again, 2 Corinthians, from somewhere in Macedonia on his way back to Corinth. So this would correspond with Acts 20:1. He soon arrived back in Corinth, and it was here that he wrote his great letter to the church in Rome. This would correspond with Acts 20:2; Corinth is not specifically mentioned here, but it would have been included in the term *Greece*. Since these six letters were written during his missionary journeys, they are sometimes called the Journey Epistles.

In the closing chapters of Acts, we are told that Paul was arrested (on a false charge) in Jerusalem and was eventually sent to Rome to be tried by the emperor himself. The book of Acts ends with Paul in chains for two years (in his own rented house, 28:30–31), and during this time he wrote four more letters. The exact chronological order here is not clear, but the four letters, classified as Prison Epistles, are Ephesians, Colossians, Philippians, and Philemon. Ephesians and Colossians are quite similar in much of their content, so they were probably written about the same time. In both Philippians and Philemon, Paul hints that he expects his imminent release from prison, so they seem to be written about the same time, toward the end of his two-year imprisonment.

For some reason, Paul was released from prison and continued his ministry. This happened after the close of the book of Acts. During this time he wrote letters to two of his good friends and colleagues—Timothy and Titus. A couple of years later, Paul was arrested again because of his ministry for Jesus Christ and imprisoned again in Rome. During this second imprisonment, he wrote his last letter, 2 Timothy. In this letter, he indicates that he knows his ministry and life are soon to come to an end. These final three letters are classified as the Pastoral Epistles, since Timothy and Titus were in pastoral ministry and Paul was writing to help and encourage them in their ministries.

James seems to be the first General Epistle written. As a matter of fact, it is likely that James was the first of all New Testament documents to be written. Hebrews, 1 and 2 Peter, and Jude were probably written about the same time that Paul was first imprisoned in Rome. John's three letters (along with his gospel and the book of Revelation) were the last New Testament documents to be written, during the last two decades of the first century.

The table that follows summarizes this information and supplies approximate dates for the writing of the books of the New Testament.

FUN FACT

The longest title of any New Testament book is found in one manuscript of the book of Revelation: "The Revelation of the all-glorious Evangelist, bosom friend [of Jesus], virgin, beloved to Christ, John the theologian, son of Salome and Zebedee, but adopted son of Mary the Mother of God, and Son of Thunder"[1] What a title!

Writing of the Books of the New Testament

Gospels	History	Epistles	Prophecy
Matthew (60s?)	Acts (62)		Revelation (90s)
Mark (50s?)			
Luke (early 60s)			
John (80s–90s)			

Pauline

Canonical	Chronological
To churches	**After 1st journey**
Romans	Galatians (48–49)
1 Corinthians	
2 Corinthians	**During 2nd journey**
Galatians	1 Thessalonians (50–51)
Ephesians	2 Thessalonians (51–52)
Philippians	
Colossians	**During 3rd journey**
1 Thessalonians	1 Corinthians (54–55)
2 Thessalonians	2 Corinthians (55–56)
	Romans (56–57)
To individuals	
1 Timothy	**1st imprisonment**
2 Timothy	Ephesians (60–62)
Titus	Colossians (60–62)
Philemon	Philippians (62)
	Philemon (62)
	Between imprisonments
	1 Timothy (62–64)
	Titus (62–64)
	2nd imprisonment
	2 Timothy (64–67)

General

Canonical	Chronological
Hebrews	James (mid-40s)
James	
1 Peter	Hebrews (60s)
2 Peter	
1 John	1 Peter (early 60s)
2 John	
3 John	2 Peter (mid-60s)
Jude	
	Jude (mid-60s)
	1–3 John (80s–90s)

Who Wrote
the New Testament?

Like the authors of the Old Testament, the New Testament authors should also be considered prophets. But more specifically, they were either apostles or closely related to an apostle. An apostle is a person who is sent out as a spokesperson and is given the authority of the one who sent him. A present-day example is the secretary of state, who is sent to speak to world leaders as the representative of the president with the very authority of the president. The apostles of the New Testament were sent out by Jesus Christ to speak for him with his delegated authority. That makes this responsibility an immensely important and influential one. It was also rather exclusive; there seem to be only thirteen that qualified: the eleven disciples of Jesus (after the death of Judas, his betrayer), Matthias (the replacement for Judas, Acts 1:15–26), and Paul, who identifies himself as an apostle in most of his letters.

All four gospels are anonymous, but ancient tradition holds that their titles—the gospel of Matthew, the gospel of Mark, the gospel of

Luke, and the gospel of John—accurately indicate their authors. Two of these were apostles: Matthew and John. They are both mentioned in Matthew 10:1–4, along with the rest of Jesus' twelve apostles.

Matthew was a tax collector when he was called by Jesus (Matthew 9:9; 10:3). Then, as now, that vocation was not very popular (to put it lightly), as the phrase "tax collectors and sinners" (Matthew 9:11) indicates. They were notorious for being dishonest and greedy, not that Matthew in particular was characterized in this way.

John, along with his brother James and father, Zebedee, was a fisherman (Matthew 4:21). He is also known as the beloved disciple, based on references such as John 13:23 and 21:20, indicating that he was probably the closest personal friend Jesus had among his disciples.

John is also the author of three letters—1, 2, and 3 John—and the last book of the New Testament—Revelation. He is not named in any of his letters. The author of 1 John does refer to himself as an eyewitness of Jesus in 1:1–3 and 4:14, which would imply that he was an apostle. In the first verses of 2 and 3 John, the author refers to himself as "the elder," probably a reference to his pastoral responsibilities, although it could also refer to the fact that he was an old man. John would have been quite old when these letters were written. There are numerous similarities in vocabulary and themes between these three letters and the gospel of John, and ancient tradition is in agreement that these letters were written by John. Unlike the gospel and 1, 2, and 3 John, the book of Revelation clearly names John as the author (1:1, 4, 9; 22:8).

The authors of the other two gospels—Mark and Luke—were not apostles, but according to tradition, they were closely associated with the apostles. Although they weren't related, Peter refers to Mark as his son in 1 Peter 5:13, indicating how close he felt to him. Scholars also believe there are hints of Peter's influence within the gospel of Mark, such as vivid retellings of events when Peter was present but Mark was not. All of this supports the very early testimony of Christian leaders that Peter was the apostolic author- ity behind the gospel of Mark. This means that Peter used his own authority as an apostle to vouch for Mark and his message. Not much is known about Mark other than that he was also known as John Mark; he was a Jew who lived in the city of Jerusalem (Acts 12:12); and he accompanied Paul and Barnabas on their first mis- sionary journey (Acts 13:5, where he is referred to only as John).

The early Christian leaders were in agreement that Luke wrote the third gospel and that Paul was the apostolic authority behind it. Paul sends greetings from Luke in Colossians 4:14, where he refers to him as "the doctor." He also refers to Luke in 2 Timothy 4:11 and Philemon 24. Obviously, Luke was a close companion to Paul. Luke acknowledged that the events he recorded in his gospel were from eyewitness accounts (Luke 1:1–4), implying that he himself was not an eyewitness. Ethnically, Luke was a Greek, making him the only Gentile author of any New Testament books.

The book of Acts is also anonymous. But the first two verses state that the author had previously written a gospel addressed to Theophilus, to whom the gospel of Luke is addressed (Luke 1:3). So there is a clear link between the gospel of Luke and the book of Acts, and ancient Christian tradition held that Luke is the author of both.

Paul wrote thirteen of the Epistles, which is more books of the New Testament than any other author. He is second only to Jesus in importance to Christianity. He was a Jew, but was raised out- side of Palestine in the city of Tarsus, in Asia Minor. His Jewish name was Saul, after the first king of Israel who was, like Paul, from the tribe of Benjamin. Paul was his Roman name. When he was around thirteen, he was sent to Jerusalem to study under the famous rabbi Gamaliel (Acts 22:3). As a Jew and a Pharisee, he was highly devoted to the Mosaic law, and came to hate Jesus Christ, Christians, and Christianity in general (Philippians 3:5–6). He was responsible for some of the early persecution of Christians, until he encountered the resurrected, glorified Christ on the road to

Damascus. He believed in Christ immediately, and the rest of his life was devoted to proclaiming the gospel of Christ, specifically to Gentiles, and establishing churches throughout the Roman Empire (Acts 9:1–30; Galatians 1:11–17). Paul rightly regarded himself as one of the apostles, but the least of them due to his former persecution of the church (1 Corinthians 15:9).

In addition to being the apostolic authority behind the gospel of Mark, the apostle Peter wrote two letters: 1 and 2 Peter. He is also known as Simon (Matthew 4:18) and Levi (Mark 2:14; Luke 5:27). Like John, he was a fisherman by trade. Jesus called him and his brother Andrew to be his disciples (Matthew 4:18–19). It is worth noting that Peter and John, two simple, uneducated fishermen, impressed the highly educated Jewish leaders with their boldness and knowledge as they defended the gospel of Jesus Christ (Acts 4:13).

Two New Testament books were written by blood relatives of Jesus: his half-brothers James and Jude. They are both mentioned in Matthew 13:55 and Mark 6:3 (Jude is called Judas). They were apparently in the upper room on the day of Pentecost (Acts 2:10-14). James, known as James the Just, was one of the leaders in the early church in Jerusalem (Acts 12:17; 15:13; Galatians 1:18–19; 2:9, 12). Little is known about Jude.

The book of Hebrews is anonymous. There has been much speculation about the author (for example, Paul, Barnabas, Luke, Apollos), but it is probably best to leave it a mystery.

FUN FACT

James and Jude did not believe that their older brother was really the Messiah (John 7:5). It was not until after his resurrection that James and probably Jude were convinced and believed (1 Corinthians 15:7). According to tradition, James was executed for his faith in Jesus.

For Whom Was
the New Testament Written?

As was true for the books of the Old Testament, the books of the New Testament are intended for all people, since this is the Word of God to humanity in general. But again, from the perspective of the human authors, these books had a more specific audience and purpose at the time of their writing. The books of the New Testament were for Christians. They are not primarily evangelistic, that is, to convince unbelievers to believe, although they certainly can be used that way. Rather, they were primarily written to inform those who already believed in Jesus Christ as their Savior what they must know and believe and how to live as a result.

The Gospels had specific ethnic audiences in the first century AD. Matthew was written for Jews. Mark was written for Romans. Luke was written for Greeks. These were the three main ethnic groups in the Roman Empire at that time, so it makes sense that God would inspire books to communicate the good news of Jesus

Christ to these people. The gospel of John does not seem to be so narrowly focused; it has a more universal audience in view—for example, "*Whoever* believes in [Jesus] shall not perish but have eternal life" (3:16). Luke has a brief and general purpose statement at the beginning of his gospel: "so that you may know the certainty of the things you have been taught" (1:4). John has a fuller and more specific purpose, but he puts it at the end of his gospel: "But these are written that you may believe that Jesus is the Messiah, the Son of God, and that by believing you may have life in his name" (20:31). All the Gospels were written to teach their readers about the life, teachings, death, and resurrection of Jesus Christ with the intention of deepening their faith in him.

The gospel of Luke and the book of Acts were addressed to a specific individual: Theophilus (Luke 1:3; Acts 1:1). Some think this was a code word for Christian, because it literally means "God-lover." However, it is probably best to assume this was a specific Greek person who was important (he is referred to as "most excellent" in Luke 1:3) and who was probably a new Christian. Perhaps he was the sponsor of Luke's research for the gospel and for the book of Acts. But regardless of these particulars, both of these books were intended for a broader audience than one individual.

Paul wrote some of his letters to churches and some to individuals. Most of the ones he wrote to churches were to those he had founded, or at least established. The exceptions to this would be Romans and probably Colossians.

His letters to individuals were 1 and 2 Timothy, Titus, and Philemon. Timothy and Titus were close fellow-workers with Paul. They were involved in pastoral ministry—Timothy in Ephesus and Titus on the island of Crete—and Paul was writing to encourage and help them in this ministry (1 Timothy 3:14–15). Philemon was a Christian who lived in the town of Colossae. Paul's purpose in this letter was to ask Philemon to accept and forgive one of his slaves, Onesimus, who had escaped, encountered Paul when he was in prison, and become a Christian (vv. 10, 17–18). This seems to be an illustration of the forgiveness and restoration that we receive from God through Jesus.

Paul's general purpose in all of these letters was to teach the Christians what to believe (truth) and how to live (holiness). He often came at this negatively by pointing out misunderstanding and false teaching that they were *not* to believe and sinful ways in which they were *not* to live. This general purpose applies not only to Paul's letters but also to the rest of the New Testament Epistles.

Among the General Epistles (those not written by Paul), Hebrews and James seem to have been written to Jewish Christians. The audience of Hebrews is not specifically stated, but the content indicates that he was writing to Jewish Christians who were being persecuted because of their Christian faith and were now on the verge of reverting back to Judaism. The writer (whoever he was) tried to persuade them to continue trusting in Christ, who is the fulfillment of Judaism. James 1:1 indicates the ethnicity of his audience when he begins, "To the twelve tribes scattered among the nations." His assumption, however, was that they were believers in Jesus.

First and Second Peter and Jude were written to Christians in general. Peter wrote his first letter "to God's elect, exiles scattered throughout" the Roman Empire (1:1). He wrote his second letter "to those who through the righteousness of our God and Savior Jesus Christ have received a faith as precious as ours" (1:1). Jude likewise wrote his letter "to those who have been called, who are loved in God the Father and kept for Jesus Christ" (v. 1). These are all simply different ways of referring to any and all Christians.

In addition to his gospel, John wrote three letters and the book of Revelation. First John, however, seems to be more like a written sermon than a letter. It has no specific address at all, but based on his other two letters and the book of Revelation, it was probably sent initially to the churches in Asia Minor to whom John ministered in the latter part of his life. Second John is addressed "to the lady chosen by God and to her children" (v. 1). There has been much debate about to whom or to what this refers. It is possible that it refers to a specific Christian woman and her children who lived in Asia Minor. But it is probably more likely that this is a reference to one of the churches in that area and the individual Christians that made up that church. "[T]he children of your sister, who is chosen by God" (v. 13) probably refers to the Christians in the church where John was when he wrote this letter. Third John is addressed "to my dear friend Gaius" (v. 1). Gaius was a common name in the first century, but this Gaius seems to be a disciple of John and possibly a pastor or elder in one of the churches in Asia Minor.

The book of Revelation is specifically addressed "to the seven churches in the province of Asia" (1:4). These are representative of all churches of Jesus Christ. Chapters 2 and 3 contain seven letters from Christ to each of these churches individually. The rest of the book was written for these Christians specifically because they were being persecuted and needed to know what the end of God's program held: victory for God and all his people through Jesus Christ. This was intended to encourage them to endure through the threat of false teaching and persecution in the present in light of God's great promises for the future.

FUN FACT

Even though the letters of the New Testament were addressed to specific people, these people were not possessive of them. The original recipients very quickly recognized the significance of these letters, copied them, and sent them to other churches so that those Christians, too, could benefit from the great truths contained in them.

What Will I Find
in the Gospels?

The word *gospel* comes from the Greek word meaning "good news." That accurately summarizes the content of Matthew, Mark, Luke, and John: the good news of the arrival and work of the Son of God, Jesus Christ. Figuring out the exact genre of these four books has been a bit of a challenge for scholars. They are not quite history, since they focus on one main character. But yet they are not quite biography, since they don't include certain aspects of a person's life that you would expect in a biography. For example, there is hardly anything regarding Jesus' childhood. Some scholars suggest that these are Greco-Roman or Hellenistic biographies, which are more limited in their coverage of a person's life. Other scholars suggest that the appropriate genre of the Gospels is gospel! In other words, these four books are really unique enough in ancient literature that they deserve a genre of their own.

Like all ancient history, but unlike modern history, what we find in the Gospels is more than "just the facts." As we have seen with Old Testament history, ancient historians were writing with an agenda. They were trying to persuade their readers of a certain viewpoint. In the case of the four gospels, this viewpoint was that Jesus was exactly who he claimed to be—the Messiah, the Son of God. This goal did not cause them to distort the facts. They were truthful and accurate in what they recorded. But they selectively chose what to include and how to package it in order to convince their audience. John's purpose statement is pretty straightforward: "But these are written that you may believe that Jesus is the Messiah, the Son of God, and that by believing you may have life in his name" (John 20:31). The gospel writers believed that a person's eternal destiny hung on believing in the person they were writing about.

As we might expect, there is a lot of overlap in the contents of the Gospels. Matthew, Mark, and Luke are the most alike, and are therefore called the Synoptic Gospels, meaning "from a common perspective." The book of John is unique. So why did God give us four gospels? Wouldn't one be enough? A part of the answer is in that word *perspective*. Even though the Synoptic Gospels have a common perspective, they are not exactly the same. Because of this we have four different angles on Jesus' life, including different emphases and some different events. The advantage of these multiple perspectives is that they help fill out our understanding of the most important person who ever lived.

It is helpful to keep in mind some basics about these four gospels as we read them. These will help us make more sense of what we read. So, let's look briefly at the authors, their original audiences, what each emphasizes about Jesus (their portrait), and a key word and verse of their text.

Matthew was a Jew and a tax collector. His vocation is noteworthy because he includes more content about money than any other gospel. That's his world. His ethnicity is noteworthy because he is writing to his own people—the Jews. This gospel is very Jewish in flavor, including a lot of their laws, customs, and concerns. Matthew's portrait of Jesus fits with his intended audience: Jesus is the messianic king. This makes sense because the Jews were waiting for the promised Messiah, and Matthew identifies that messiah as none other than Jesus. A key word might be *fulfilled*. What is one of the best ways to convince a Jewish audience that Jesus is the Messiah? By demonstrating the fact from their own Scriptures. And so, over and over, Matthew quotes from or alludes to Old Testament messianic prophecies and then shows how Jesus fulfilled them. One of the best examples is the virgin birth of Jesus to Mary, as prophesied in Isaiah 7:14 and quoted by Matthew in 1:22–23. A key verse is Matthew 5:17, where Jesus says, "Do not think that I have come to abolish the Law or the Prophets [the Old Testament]; I have not come to abolish them but to *fulfill* them."

Mark was also a Jew, but his vocation is unknown. He may have been from a prosperous family who lived in Jerusalem. The early church apparently met in the house of Mark's parents (Acts 12:12), which implies it must have been sizeable. Mark's audience is generally understood to be Roman. Why do we think so? There are some clues in the book that point in this direction. First of all, the audience doesn't appear to be Jewish. For example, in 7:3–4, Mark provides a parenthetical explanation of the Jewish custom of ceremonial washing. This explanation would have been unnecessary for a Jewish audience. Other clues seem to point toward a Roman audience. For example, in the context of the offering of a poor widow (12:41–44), Mark converts Jewish coinage ("small copper coins," from the Greek word *lepta*) to Roman coinage ("penny," or "a few cents," from the Greek translation of the Latin *quadrans*). That was necessary so the audience would get the point of the story.

Mark's portrait of Jesus is as a humble servant. He emphasizes that he came to serve others. The key verse might be what Jesus said in 10:45, "For even the Son of Man did not come to be served, but to serve, and to give his life as a ransom for many." Accordingly, Mark records more of what Jesus did than what he said; his focus is on the practical side of Jesus. A key word supports this: *immediately,* which shows up eleven times in this gospel. This and other words, like *then,* provide a sense of urgency and immediacy regarding what Jesus was doing. All of this would be impressive to Romans.

Luke is the only Gentile author of any New Testament book. More specifically, he was Greek. He was a doctor (Colossians 4:14), which suggests education and intelligence. His primary audience, not surprisingly, was his own people, the Greeks. He worked alongside Paul planting churches among the Greeks, so it makes sense that he would want to present a gospel specifically designed for them. Luke's portrait of Jesus is as a perfect human being, and so he emphasized the true humanity of Jesus. This would appeal to ancient Greeks, who were the philosophical type and thought a lot about what perfect humanity was all about. A key phrase is *Son of Man,* which is used in one of the book's key verses: "For the Son of Man came to seek and to save the lost" (19:10).

John was a Jew and a fisherman by trade, an uneducated laborer. His audience does not seem to be as specific as the other gospels. Instead, it is for all people in general—"For God so loved *the world*" (3:16). John's portrait of Jesus is as the Son of God; he emphasized the full deity of Jesus. The key word of this book is simple: *believe.* John emphasizes belief or faith (or lack of it) in Jesus throughout this gospel. A key verse is "But these are written that you may believe that Jesus is the Christ, the Son of God, and that by believing you may have life in his name" (20:31 NIV 1984).

	Matthew	*Mark*	*Luke*	*John*
Author	Jew; tax collector	Jew; prosperous (?)	Greek; doctor	Jew; fisherman
Audience	Jews	Romans	Greeks (Gentiles)	everyone
Portrait	messianic king	humble servant	perfect humanity	Son of God
Key Word/ Phrase	*fulfilled*	*immediately*	*Son of Man*	*believe*
Key Verse	5:17	10:45	19:10	20:31

FUN FACT

None of the gospel writers identifies himself as the author of his own book; the books themselves are anonymous. The authorship of the Gospels is based on ancient trustworthy Christian tradition.

What Will I Find in the Book of Acts?

A cts is really the second volume of Luke's two-volume work, with the gospel of Luke being the first volume (compare the opening verses of each book). Therefore, if the gospel is about what "Jesus *began* to do and to teach" (Acts 1:1), the book of Acts is about what Jesus *continued* to do and teach, but now through his followers, and even more specifically, through the work of the Holy Spirit. The Holy Spirit really is the primary character in the story told here, as evident through references to the Spirit throughout the book.

Luke's purpose in the book of Acts seems to be to demonstrate how God moved the good news of Jesus Christ, the gospel, from its geographical roots in Jerusalem, farther and farther out to the city of Rome, the capital of the Roman Empire. In other words, now that the incarnate Son of God had provided the way for all people to be made right with God, God was determined to get the message of Jesus Christ out to all people by moving it from the center of the Jewish world to the center of the Gentile world. This intention is indicated by a key verse of the book, Acts 1:8—"But you will receive power when the Holy Spirit comes on you; and you will be my witnesses in Jerusalem, and in all Judea and Samaria, and to the ends of the earth."

This can be seen throughout the book in several ways. First, we see it in a series of four events that demonstrate the progressive advance of the gospel. Step one is recorded in Acts 8:4–25, as the gospel moves out from its roots among Jews and into Samaria. Samaritan worship looked very Jewish; they worshiped the God of Israel and followed the Old Testament Law. However, they were hated by the Jews due to their mixed ancestry; they were "half-breeds," the descendants of Jewish and Gentile intermarriage dating back to the Old Testament period. This ethnic antipathy was a major hurdle, even for Jewish Christians, so God had to launch a persecution against the Christians to push them out of Jerusalem and among the despised Samaritans (8:1). Once the gospel was presented to them, many Samaritans believed in Jesus Christ (8:12). One major hurdle for the gospel had been crossed.

The second step is recorded in the latter part of chapter 8. After his great success in proclaiming the gospel among the Samaritans, God redirected Philip to do the same for one individual on the edge of nowhere (8:26). The Ethiopian eunuch was coming from Jerusalem where he had gone to worship the God of Israel at the temple. Even though it is not explicit in the text, this indicates that he was at least a *God-fearer,* a term applied to a Gentile who believed like and worshiped as a Jew but who had not officially converted to Judaism; he may even have been an official convert to Judaism, called a *proselyte.* On his way home, he was reading the book of Isaiah, specifically the amazing chapter 53, which is about the coming messiah. God brought Philip along his path to help him understand the fulfillment of that prophecy in Jesus (8:35). As a result, this man believed and was baptized (8:36–38). The man was a Gentile from Ethiopia, which at that time was considered to be the southern limitation of civilization. This was an early fulfillment of the gospel going to "the ends of the earth" (1:8).

The third step is recorded in chapter 10. Peter was led by God through a vision (10:9–19) to the house of Cornelius, a Roman army officer. He, too, was a full-blooded Gentile ethnically, but is also identified in the text as "God-fearing" (10:2), one who believed like and worshiped as a Jew. As a result of Peter's sharing the gospel with Cornelius and his household, they believed in Jesus and were baptized (10:44–48). Whereas the conversion of the Ethiopian eunuch anticipated the gospel going to the edge of the Roman Empire, the conversion of Cornelius anticipated its going to the capital of the Roman Empire, Rome.

The fourth and final step is recorded in chapter 16. Paul was led to the continent of Europe through a vision (16:9–10). In the city of Philippi he and Silas were thrown into prison, but through a God-sent earthquake they had the opportunity to answer the jailer's famous question, "What must I do to be saved?" (16:30). The simplest gospel is found in their answer: "Believe in the Lord Jesus, and you will be saved" (16:31). This man, like the Ethiopian Eunuch and Cornelius, was a full-blooded Gentile, but he had no apparent connection with Judaism at all; he was a pagan.

So from the roots of Christianity among full-blooded Jews, God propelled the gospel to the Samaritans, who were half-Jew/half-Gentile and worshiped the God of Israel, to full-blooded Gentiles, who were also worshiping as Jews—one representing the extent of the empire, the other representing the heart of the empire—and finally, to a full-blooded Gentile who did not worship the God of Israel at all. God had pushed the good news of Jesus Christ to those who needed to hear it in the fully pagan world.

A second way Luke demonstrates the progression of the gospel is through the evangelistic journeys of Paul recorded in the latter part of Acts, beginning in chapter 13. These three trips cover more and more territory as Paul took the gospel to places where Christ had not yet been named (Romans 15:20). At the close of the book of Acts, Paul was imprisoned in Rome, but he continued to proclaim the gospel (28:30–31). Even though its messenger was in chains, the gospel message itself could never be put in chains, as Paul revealed in Philippians 1:12–14. God saw to it that the gospel reached the heart of the empire.

The story of Acts continues—"Acts 29," as some people have called it—as God is still propelling the gospel of Jesus Christ to all the peoples of the world.

FUN FACT

As with his gospel, Luke does not identify himself as the author of the book of Acts, nor does he even mention himself by name as a character in the book. However, he does include himself indirectly several times by saying "we" or "us" (Acts 16:10, 17; 20:5-6; 27:1). We know from a few of Paul's letters that Luke was there at times working with Paul (Colossians 4:14; Philemon 24).

What Will I Find in the Epistles?

As we have said, the word *epistle* is simply the Greek word for "letter." The New Testament epistles are generally letters to churches or individuals. There are twenty-one of them, and they make up about a third of the New Testament. Thirteen are written by the apostle Paul, and the rest, categorized as General Epistles, are written by a variety of authors: James, Peter, John, Jude, and the unknown author of Hebrews.

These letters are also called "occasional literature." The word *occasional* here does not mean "every now and then," but rather that something specific prompted the authors of the letters to write them. From the occasion, then, comes the purpose of the letter. But the occasion and the purpose are not normally stated within the letter itself, which makes sense, because the recipients would have known what was going on among them and why the author was writing about it. However, as present-day readers, we don't have that insider information, so it is helpful to try to figure it out. It is not usually very hard. It's like listening to one end of a phone conversation—even though you are missing half of it, it is usually pretty clear what is being discussed. So in the epistles, we have to read between the lines and determine as best we can the occasion and the purpose. These purposes generally fall into two broad categories: (1) teaching or clarifying what Christians should know and believe; and (2) addressing a problem or problems.

The form of the New Testament epistles was the standard form of letters at that time. The first part was the salutation or greeting. Here the author identifies himself and his recipients—"from so and so, to so and so" (see Colossians 1:1–2). Paul would normally add the greeting "grace and peace" (Colossians 1:2). "Peace" came from his Jewish heritage: *shalom*. "Grace" was the standard Greek greeting, essentially something like "I hope you are doing well." Of course, Paul understood there was more to the word *grace* than just that!

The second part of the epistle was an expression of thanks or a commendation: "I am thankful for so and so" or "I applaud you for such and such." For Paul, this was usually in the form of a prayer of thanksgiving to God, thanking him for the faith, hope, and love given to and found among the Christians in that particular church (see Colossians 1:3–8).

The third part of the epistle comprises the main body or content of the letter (1:9–4:9). The contents of the epistles generally fall into the following broad categories.

The first is theology or doctrine—what Christians are to believe. For example, in his second letter, Peter was alarmed at the looming threat of false teaching. He wrote, "But there were also false prophets among the people, just as there will be false teachers among you. They will secretly introduce destructive heresies" (2 Peter 2:1). He prepared his readers for this danger by reminding them of the truth they had been taught (1:12–15; 3:1–2) so that they could identify false teaching and reject it (3:17–18). In

1 Thessalonians, Paul had to deal with misunderstandings regarding what he had taught about the second coming of Christ. The Thessalonians did understand that they were to have a daily expectation of the return of Christ. However, they did not understand how Christians who died before the return of Christ would be affected. They thought deceased Christians would miss out on that glorious event. So Paul wrote, "Brothers and sisters, we do not want you to be uninformed about those who sleep in death, so that you do not grieve like the rest of mankind, who have no hope" (1 Thessalonians 4:13). He then went on to clarify that Christians who have died are actually going to accompany Christ back to earth when he returns (4:14).

The second content category is how Christians are to live: ethics or morality. For example, the early Christian often faced persecution, which also threatened their unity. So Paul (who was in prison himself due to persecution) wrote to the Philippian church, "Whatever happens, conduct yourselves in a manner worthy of the gospel of Christ. Then . . . I will know that you stand firm in the one Spirit, striving together as one for the faith of the gospel without being frightened in any way by those who oppose you" (Philippians 1:27–28). Immorality was a major problem among the early Gentile Christians because of their pagan and permissive backgrounds, especially so in the "sin city" of the ancient world, Corinth. So Paul wrote to them, "Flee from sexual immorality" because "your bodies are temples of the Holy Spirit" (1 Corinthians 6:18–20).

The order of these two content categories is important, especially in the letters of Paul. His assumption, which is absolutely correct, is that how we live flows out of what we believe. Therefore, if what we believe is incorrect or incomplete, our Christian behavior will be deficient. On the other hand, if what we believe is true and right, our Christian behavior will be healthy and pleasing to God. One of the best examples of this is Paul's letter to the

Ephesians. It divides nicely into halves. Chapters 1–3 are doctrinal—what Christians are to know and believe. He told them that they were dead in their sins but were now alive with Christ and *in Christ* (an important phrase in these chapters). Chapters 4–6 are practical—how Christians are to live *because* they are alive in Christ. He transitioned from the application of the doctrine by saying, "As a prisoner for the Lord, then, I urge you to live a life worthy of the calling you have received" (4:1), and that calling was what he had discussed in the previous chapters. Paul's letter to the Romans is another example. Chapters 1–11 contain amazing, deep, important, and significant theology that Christians should know and believe. He begins to apply that theology in 12:1, when he says, "Therefore, I urge you, brothers and sisters, in view of God's mercy [a good succinct summary of chapters 1–11], to offer your bodies as a living sacrifice, holy and pleasing to God." Romans 12–16, then, provide more specific application for the Christian life.

The fourth part of the epistle to the Colossians contains greetings from and to specific individuals (4:10–17).

The fifth and final part is the closing. For Paul, that was generally "Grace be with you" (4:18). Paul begins his letters with grace and ends them with grace. This captures Paul's great emphasis with regard to the gospel of Jesus Christ: It is all of God's grace—freely given!

FUN FACT

Not all the books that fit into the category of Epistles reflect this form. Hebrews ends like a letter but doesn't start like one. First John does neither; it is probably a written sermon rather than a letter per se.

What Will I Find in the Book of Revelation?

This book is one of the most challenging in the Bible because of the type of literature it is. The title of the book can be literally translated: "The Apocalypse to John." The apostle John is the human author (1:1, 4, 9). But the first verse adds that it is also the "apocalypse of Jesus Christ." The Greek word *apocalypse* means "revealing" or "uncovering." So the content of this book was revealed by Jesus Christ and recorded by the apostle John (1:1–3).

This book, then, falls into the category of apocalyptic literature. That places it within a body of Jewish literature that was written between about 200 BC and AD 100, a period of time when the Jews were suffering occupation and persecution at the hands of Gentiles. Because of these hard times, the Jews were wondering about the great promises in the Old Testament prophets regarding the coming of the Messiah and the glories of the Jewish kingdom. The fulfillment of these promises seemed very remote and the Jews were discouraged. This body of literature was produced to remind the Jews that although times were tough, God's promises would be fulfilled.

These are the characteristics of apocalyptic literature: (1) the ending of the present age, which is characterized by evil; that is, the culmination of the age-old war between good and evil, God and Satan; (2) the resurrection and final judgment of all people; (3) the transformation of the universe with the effects of sin being removed; (4) the ushering in of a new age—the messianic kingdom; (5) this taking place through a cataclysmic intervention of God into human history and the physical realm; and (6) usually communicated through visions, symbolism, and imagery, often of a rather bizarre nature, as in a bad dream.

A few Old Testament prophetic books, such as the latter half of Daniel and parts of Ezekiel and Zechariah, were written before the period of apocalyptic literature, but some of its characteristics were anticipated in them. As a matter of fact, the book of Revelation cannot be understood apart from this Old Testament background, especially the book of Daniel.

Many of the characteristics of apocalyptic literature are also seen in the book of Revelation, but there are also a few differences between Revelation and other such literature. Apocalyptic literature falsely (pseudonymously) named great Old Testament characters as the authors, such as Moses, Enoch, or Ezra. However, John accurately identifies himself as the author of Revelation. Apocalyptic literature was normally pessimistic about the present and optimistic about the future. While Revelation is realistic about the challenges for the people of God in the present, it is optimistic about both the present and the future due to the successful work of Jesus Christ at his first coming.

The purpose of the book of Revelation is stated in the first verse: "to show his servants what must soon take place." This was intended to encourage Christians, especially in times of persecution and hardship. John personally understood this, since he was persecuted by the Roman emperor Domitian. In fact, he wrote this book while in exile on the island of Patmos (1:9). Knowing what

God has promised for the future helps God's people live rightly in the present, especially during challenging times.

Revelation 1:19 may tip us off to the structure of the book: "Write, therefore, [1] what you have seen, [2] what is now and [3] what will take place later." After the introduction (1:1–8), the first main section (1:9–20) is "what you see," namely, an amazing vision of the resurrected, glorified Jesus Christ. The second section is "what is now" in the *present* (2:1–3:22). Here we have letters from Jesus Christ to seven churches in Asia Minor, John's original audience (1:4). These were churches in and around the area of Ephesus that John knew well, since, according to tradition, he oversaw these churches at the end of his life. The Christians who made up these churches were dealing with persecution, temptation, false teaching, and more. They represented what Christians of all times struggle with, thus the need for encouragement (and warning!). The third section is "what must take place after this" in the *future* (4:1–22:5). This is the bulk of the book that records John's visions of what is to come. The book ends with a grand conclusion (22:6–21).

The main section of the book (4:1–22:5) can be broken down a bit further. Chapters 4 and 5 record what John saw as he was swept up in a vision into heaven. He saw God on the throne being worshiped by angelic beings, and the Lamb, Jesus Christ, was given a scroll with seven (a symbolic number) seals, which he alone was worthy to open (5:9).

Revelation 6:1–8:1 reveals what happens after each seal is broken: There is some form of divine judgment against sin. These judgments are followed by another set of seven divine judgments, described as the blowing of trumpets (8:2–11:19). In chapters 12:1–14:20, we witness a symbolic vision of the war between God, his angels, and his people on the one hand, and the enemies of God on the other—a red dragon, who is Satan, and his allies, a beast coming out of the sea, and another beast coming out of the earth. A final set of seven divine judgments described as plagues are recorded in

15:1–16:21. The divine destruction of Babylon (perhaps symbolic of the oppressive rule of Rome at that time) is noted in 17:1–18:24. The scene then switches to heaven (19:10), where there is great rejoicing over this just judgment of God. But the final and greatest judgment follows: 19:11–20:10 describe the return of Jesus Christ, his victory over all his enemies, and his reign on the earth for a thousand years. God's final judgment of sin, the great white throne, is explained in 20:11–15. Finally, eternity—"a new heaven and a new earth" and "the new Jerusalem"—is described in 21:1–22:5.

This book is indeed a challenge to understand because of all the symbols and imagery. However, despite the difficulties in interpreting the details of the book, the main theme is crystal clear: God *will* be victorious over all that opposes him (sin, sinners, Satan) through Jesus Christ, and the righteous *will* share in that great victory and enjoy God in his presence for all eternity. In the meantime, the great present hope of believers is our Lord's emphatic promise: "Look, I am coming soon! (22:7, 12, 20). Therefore, the present longing of Christians is "Amen. Come, Lord Jesus" (22:20).

FUN FACT

Revelation records how God will finally put right what went wrong soon after creation through sin. Note the connections between the book of Genesis and the book of Revelation. Here are a few interesting examples: Genesis 1:1: "heavens and the earth" and Revelation 21:1: "a new heaven and a new earth"; the sun and the moon for light (Genesis 1:14-19) and God and his Son for light (Revelation 21:23); the arrival of sin (Genesis 3:1-6) and the removal of sin (Revelation 21:8); banishment from the tree of life (Genesis 3:22) and access to the tree of life (Revelation 22:2). The story is complete.

What Does *the Canon* Mean, and How Were the Books Chosen to Complete It?

The English word *canon* has its roots in the Hebrew language. The word *qaneh* refers to a reed or swamp plant that was used as a measuring device. From there it came into the Greek language as *kanōn* and into the English language as *canon*, where it means a standard by which something is measured. Eventually, the word came to be applied to the books of the Bible that have been recognized as the Word of God.

The ancient Jews had a sizeable volume of religious literature in the Hebrew language, as did the early Christians in the Greek language. Both Jews and Christians understood that not all of these books qualified as God's Word, so they needed to recognize which belonged in the canon and which did not. Notice I did *not* say, they needed to *determine* which were God's Word and which weren't. God had already determined this. His people had only to *recognize* it.

How the Jews in the Old Testament period went about this is somewhat obscure, simply because it took place so long ago and nobody was taking notes. What appears to have happened went something like this: The first five books of the Old Testament, which were written by Moses, were immediately recognized as the Word of God. Moses had gotten much of the material on Mount Sinai directly from God so there was no doubt in anyone's mind that those five books were God's own words. As the centuries passed, God worked by his Spirit through other authors to write books that were eventually recognized as the Word of God and included in the canon. The books coming after Moses' were books of history, which were categorized by the Jews as the Former Prophets. A prophet is simply a messenger of God, and God's people recognized that these historians were delivering God's message in the form of history. Later, other authors wrote, inspired by God, and their books were categorized as the Latter Prophets. These are the books that we normally think of as prophetic books—Isaiah, Jeremiah, Ezekiel, and others. Finally, the books of poetry, along with some additional books of history, were written and categorized as the Writings. The Hebrew, or Old Testament, books, then, were accepted as part of the canon in three stages: the Law (the five books of Moses), the Prophets (including Former Prophets and Latter Prophets), and the Writings.

The process of recognizing the Old Testament canon can be summarized in two terms: *gradually*—the whole process took place over a millennium; and *informally*—these books were recognized at the grassroots level by the people of God. They were, apparently, enabled by the Spirit of God to intuitively recognize the Word of God. The result was the thirty-nine books of the Old Testament. The Old Testament canon was fully accepted by Jesus and the first-century Christians.

The process of recognizing the New Testament canon was similar, although it moved along more quickly. All of the books of the New Testament were written by the end of the first century. They were generally recognized as the Word of God almost immediately. Peter showed this in his second letter: "[Paul] writes the same way in all his letters, speaking in them of these matters. His letters contain some things that are hard to understand, which ignorant and unstable people distort, as they do *the other Scriptures* [the Old Testament], to their own destruction" (2 Peter 3:16). We don't know if Peter knew he was writing the Word of God at the moment he was writing, but he knew that what Paul had written in his letters was as much the Word of God as the Old Testament. Generally, the books of the New Testament were *informally* recognized by Christians by about the middle of the second century.

A more formal recognition of the New Testament canon took place several centuries later, due to the threat of false teaching. In order to deal with error, one must establish a basis of truth on which to stand. That's what the early church leaders did in the fourth century by *formally* declaring the books of the New Testament canon. It was their way of saying, "If you claim to promote anything that does not fit with the teachings of these twenty-seven books (along with the books of the Old Testament), you are promoting heresy."

How did this more formal declaration come about? In the fourth century, several church councils met, and leaders of the church considered candidates for the canon along these lines:

Who wrote the book? It had to be an apostle, or someone closely associated with an apostle, who wrote no later than the first century.

Is it accurate and truthful? It had to conform with the Word of God that had already been recognized; it had to be doctrinally consistent and factually correct.

Is it dynamic and transformational? It had to demonstrate the power of God by having a spiritual impact on its readers.

Has it already been widely accepted by the people of God? There had already been about 300 years of Christian history behind the existing books.

The whole process was somewhat subjective, which might make us nervous to think about. We might have preferred a "canonization machine." A book would be tossed in one end and come out the other end either in the God's Word chute or the Not God's Word chute. However, the early leaders of the church had complete confidence that the Spirit of God was guiding them through the process, and He would not allow them to make a mistake. They knew that God cares greatly about his Word, and they trusted that He would protect it. Psalm 138:2 says, "For you have exalted above all things your name and your word" (NIV 1984). We, too, should have complete confidence that everything that is God's Word has been included in our Bible, and everything that is not God's Word has been left out. This has been the confidence of Christians down through the centuries.

FUN FACT

The earliest list of all twenty-seven books of the New Testament canon is in the Easter letter of Athanasius, Bishop of Alexandria, in AD 367.

In What Languages Was the Bible Written?

Almost all of the Old Testament was originally written in Hebrew, but a few parts were written in Aramaic, also known as Syriac. These include Ezra 4:8–6:18; 7:12–26; Daniel 2:4–7:28; and a few other isolated verses. Hebrew and Aramaic both belong to the Semitic language group (others in this group include Phoenician, Arabic, Akkadian, and Ugaritic). The term *Semitic* comes from Shem, the name of Noah's oldest son (Genesis 6:10).

The word *Hebrew* comes from the name given the Israelites by non-Israelites. The term is seen in Genesis 14:13 and 1 Samuel 4:6, for example. The Hebrew language, then, was the Israelites' native tongue for most of the Old Testament period. Hebrew is a vivid language, ideally suited to telling stories in a pictorial way. This expresses how Hebrews tended to think—more often in concrete pictures than in abstract concepts. According to Bible scholars Norman Geisler and William Nix, "Hebrew is a language through which the message is felt rather than thought."[1] That is, it is a language of the heart rather than the head. The Hebrew language proved an ideal means through which God could reveal himself through acts in history as opposed to simply making theological statements.

During the time of the Assyrian Empire (tenth through seventh centuries BC), the Assyrians' native language, Aramaic, became the trade language of much of the ancient Near East. The name itself comes from the Arameans who lived in Aram, later known as Syria (thus the term *Syriac*) located northeast of the Sea of Galilee. Aramaic continued to be the primary language throughout the Near East through the fourth century BC, when Greek began to displace it after the conquests of Alexander the Great. During their time of exile in Assyria, and later in Babylon, the Israelites began speaking Aramaic rather than Hebrew. They continued its use even after the Persians, who had defeated the Babylonians, allowed them to return home in 538 BC. This became a problem for the Jews who had returned, because they could no longer understand the Hebrew Scriptures; God's Word had to be explained to them in Aramaic. This is what was happening in Nehemiah 8:8: "They [Ezra and other Levites] read from the Book of the Law of God, making it clear and giving the meaning so that the people could understand what was being read." What was initially done orally was eventually written down and called *Targums,* the Aramaic word meaning "translations." These would be the very first translations of Scripture. The Israelites, or *Jews,* as they came to be known at this time in history, who lived in Palestine (formerly called *Canaan*), continued to speak Aramaic as their native language into the first century AD. Aramaic was the language Jesus himself learned and spoke (see Mark 15:34).

The New Testament was written in *koine,* or common Greek—that is, "street language" Greek. This is significant, in that God did not see fit to inspire the books of the New Testament to be written in academic Greek, making them accessible only to scholars. He inspired them in the common Greek, because His Word is for *all* people. Alexander the Great established the Greek Empire in the fourth century BC, and along with it, Greek as the universal language. This was so widespread that even after the Romans displaced the Greeks as the dominant power, they continued to promote Greek as the common language. As with Hebrew for the Old Testament, it is significant that God chose to use Greek to communicate the books of the New Testament. Greek is a language of the mind (remember ancient Greek philosophy). It provides technical precision, which is important in stating ideas, concepts, or thoughts. Greek is therefore ideally suited to communicate propositional or theological truth. This would be hard to do in a more pictorial language like Hebrew. It seems that God also chose Greek for the books of the New Testament since so many people spoke it in the first century. This aided in the efficient, timely communication and spread of the gospel of Jesus Christ as recorded in the books of the New Testament. Remember that Jesus commanded that disciples be made from "all nations" (Matthew 28:19).

It might be helpful to discuss one more step regarding the original languages of the Bible: the process of copying the books of the Bible. The term *autograph* is applied to the original biblical documents written by the authors or their scribes. None of these originals are *extant* today, which means "still in existence or available in a library or museum." However, there are copies available. There are fewer for the Old Testament, but *many* for the New Testament—nearly 6,000 partial or full manuscripts! In a technical sense, a copy is still in the original biblical language—Hebrew copied to Hebrew and Greek copied to Greek. Since these copies were made before the invention of the printing press, this was very tedious work, done completely by hand.

What is also important to note here is how seriously the copyists or scribes took their responsibility. They understood that this was no ordinary literature being copied; it was the very Word of God.

Consequently, they did their work with as much care as possible. Being imperfect human beings, they did not do a perfect job—there are minor differences between copies—but they were amazingly accurate. It seems that God providentially worked through them to faithfully preserve His Word as communicated initially in the autographs of Scripture.

A good example of this is the group of scribes called the Masoretes, who worked around AD 500–1000. They are well-known for their faithful and accurate copying of the Hebrew Scriptures. An example of their diligence is that they kept track of the number of lines and letters and even the very middle letter of the manuscripts they were copying. After completing a copy, which normally took months, they would compare the number of lines and letters and the middle letter of their copy to the source manuscript, and if there was any deviation, they would destroy the copy and start over. This should give us great confidence in the accuracy of the Hebrew and Greek manuscripts upon which our English Bible is based.

FUN FACT

The current Hebrew text used by biblical scholars is known as the Masoretic Text, the work of these Jewish scribes. The Dead Sea Scrolls, which were found in 1947, and predate the Masoretic Text by about 1,000 years, confirm the accuracy of the Masoretic Text and demonstrate that the Hebrew text was faithfully preserved through the centuries.

When and How
Was the Bible Translated
Into English?

Christians very quickly embarked on the task of translating the Bible into other languages. After all, even though God's Word was for all people, not all people spoke Hebrew and Greek. Jesus had commanded his followers to "go and make disciples of all nations" (Matthew 28:19), communicating the gospel to unbelievers and educating new believers in Jesus Christ; therefore, Christians understood the importance of immediately translating the Bible into the languages of the people around them. That work continues even today as many ethnic groups do not yet have the Bible, or even parts of it, in their own languages.

Probably the earliest translation of the entire Bible was the Old Latin produced in the early second century, if not the late first century. Latin was the native language of the Romans and was the marketplace language in the Western Roman Empire. The Old

Syriac translation, also known as the *Peshitta* (meaning "simple"), was produced from the middle second century to early third century. Syriac was a common marketplace language in the Eastern Roman Empire. Other important translations were created in the following centuries in Coptic (Egyptian), Gothic (early German), Ethiopic, and Arabic.

Another important reason to translate Scripture is that, since all languages evolve, there is always the need for updated, modernized versions. Even though God has blessed English speakers with many good English translations of the Bible, new translations are also legitimate because the English language has changed, sometimes dramatically. This is obvious if you try to read literature in Old English. It is almost like reading another language! So even though the King James Version of the Bible remains one of the most important and influential, the English language has seen considerable changes since 1611.

For example, in the King James Version, Philippians 1:27 reads, "Only let your conversation be as it becometh the gospel of Christ." What do you think of when you hear the word *conversation*? No doubt, what comes to mind is how we communicate, or speak, to other people. But the Greek word used here in Philippians has to do with conduct, behavior, or lifestyle, which certainly includes how we speak to others, but is much broader. The New International Version translates this verse as follows: "Whatever happens, conduct yourselves in a manner worthy of the gospel of Christ." The word *conversation* in the 1600s had the broader meaning of conduct or behavior, but now is restricted to verbal communication. So an inherent danger in using older translations is misunderstanding.

Even though there were earlier attempts at translating parts of the Bible into the English language, the first complete translation was overseen by John Wycliffe. He was a first-rate scholar and pastor who was critical of the state of the Church and the clergy in England and longed for revival among Christians there. For this to happen, they needed the Bible in their own language. The Wycliffe translation was not based on the original Hebrew and Greek texts, since they were simply not available at the time. Rather, it was based on the Latin Vulgate (meaning "vulgar" or "common"). This was an immensely important translation produced by Saint Jerome in the late fourth and early fifth centuries. It was the commonly used Bible for nearly one thousand years, and is still, as it was in Wycliffe's day, the official version used by the Roman Catholic Church. The Wycliffe Bible, then, is a translation based on a translation, which is less than ideal. It was published in the 1380s and immediately banned by the church authorities, not because it was in English, but because Wycliffe was considered to be a heretic due to his criticism of the Church and clergy.

The first English translation of the Bible to be based on the original Hebrew and Greek text was the work of William Tyndale. Like Wycliffe, he was an accomplished scholar, critical of the Church and clergy, and much opposed for his views. As a result, he had to go to Germany to finish his translation of the New Testament, which he completed in 1525. He was able to have it printed in Germany and then smuggled back into England. He continued translating the Old Testament, but before he could complete it, he was arrested, found guilty of heresy, and executed in 1536. The influence of Tyndale's work is clear in that around 90 percent of his translation continued into the King James Version and on into revisions of that version.

The work of finishing the translation of the Old Testament was carried on by a disciple of Tyndale, John Rogers, who wrote under the name Thomas Matthew. In 1537, one year after Tyndale's death, Henry VIII authorized an English translation of the Bible to be printed in England. That version was the work of Tyndale and Matthew, and was the first Bible in Modern English.

Other English translations came along in the tradition of Tyndale's work (e.g., the Great Bible, the Geneva Bible, the Bishop's Bible), but the most influential was the Authorized Version of 1611, better known as the King James Version, named for James I who authorized it. It was the first English translation to be produced by a team of noteworthy scholars. They also had the advantage of significant advances in scholarship, making it the most reliable English translation to date. It quickly became the Standard English version for the next three centuries and had a profound influence on the English language itself.

The twentieth century produced an explosion of new English translations. Some of the more well-known were intentional revisions of the King James Bible. For example, the Revised Version (1885) was created in England, and the American Standard Version (1901) and the New King James Version (1982) were created in the United States. Later translations were revisions of these revisions, such as the Revised Standard Version (1952) and the New Revised Standard Version (1989), as well as the New American Standard Version (1971) and its updated edition (1995). One of the newer translations, the English Standard Version (2001), seems to be a more evangelical alternative to the New Revised Standard Version.

Some modern versions are intentional "fresh starts," as opposed to revisions of previous translations, such as the New English Bible (1970, more non-evangelical), the New International Version (1978, more evangelical, and subsequent updates in 1984 and 2011), *God's Word Translation* (1995, evangelical), and the New English Translation (the NET Bible, 2001, evangelical). The twentieth century also introduced a new category of translations: the paraphrase. These sound very fresh and new. Examples include the New Testament in Modern English (also known as the J. B. Phillips Version, 1958, revised 1972), the Berkeley Version (1959), *The Living Bible* (1971), and *The Message: The Bible in Contemporary Language* (2002).

FUN FACT

In the early sixteenth century, Bishop Tunstall hated William Tyndale's New Testament so much that he paid someone to purchase copies to destroy them. What he did not know was that this individual was a friend of William Tyndale, and he used the money Tunstall gave him to finance the printing of more copies. For every copy that was paid for and destroyed by Tunstall, four more were produced.

Which Translation
of the Bible
Should I Use?

Any good translation of the Bible should be characterized by accuracy and clarity. *Accuracy* means that the translation correctly and precisely conveys the meaning of the Hebrew and Greek text into the target language (we will assume English). If it distorts the meaning of the biblical text, it is not a very good translation. *Clarity* means that the translation is easily understood by an English speaker. If an English speaker cannot understand it, it isn't a very good translation.

The work of translation is a challenge. A word in one language cannot always be translated with a single word in a target language. Also, languages often have different sentence structure; this is certainly true of Hebrew, Greek, and English. If translating simply meant swapping a word in one language for a word with the same meaning in another language, all translation could be accomplished by computers. That would be efficient, but it isn't realistic. It is important to find translators who are proficient in multiple languages and cultures, as well as wise in making crucial judgment calls.

Because languages vary so greatly from one another, it is hard to be completely accurate and completely clear at the same time. The translation team, then, needs to prioritize their intentions. They may decide to place the highest priority on accuracy with regard to the original languages, in which case clarity may have to suffer a bit. On the other hand, they may decide to place the highest priority on clarity with regard to their English-speaking audience, and accuracy may suffer a bit. Their decisions amount to a philosophy of translation that falls on a continuum.

At one end of the continuum, translations that prioritize accuracy and focus on the original languages are called *formal equivalence* (or *literal*, but this term can be misunderstood) translations. *Formal* means that the translators are trying to capture as closely as possible in English the "form" of the original. These are also known as word-for-word translations—this English word for this Hebrew or Greek word. Good examples are the King James Version, the New King James Version, the Revised Standard Version, the New Revised Standard Version, the New American Standard Bible, and the English Standard Version.

In the middle of the continuum, translations that prioritize clarity and focus on the target language are called either *dynamic equivalence* or *functional equivalence* translations. These translations try to capture the dynamic or function of the original text in the English translation. These translators want their translation to work for the English-speaking reader in the same way that the original Hebrew and Greek text worked for a native Hebrew or Greek speaker. These are also known as idea-for-idea or thought-for-thought translations. Good examples are the New English Bible, the New International Version, *God's Word Translation*, and the New Living Bible.

At the other end of the continuum, some translations that prioritize clarity go beyond focusing on a target language, instead focusing on a target audience (for example, children). These are called *paraphrases*. Paraphrases try to help readers understand the text rather than merely translating it. Good examples are the New Testament in Modern English, by J. B. Phillips; *The Living Bible,* produced by Ken Taylor for his children; and *The Message,* by Eugene Peterson.

Another important thing to keep in mind is that as translations move from formal equivalence translations at one end to paraphrases at the other end, more of the translators' interpretation of the biblical text creeps into the translation. There will always be *some* of this interpretation in translation because, again, no two languages are the same and translators have to make judgment calls. Formal equivalence translations minimize this. Dynamic or functional equivalence translations allow a little more interpretation for the sake of clarity. Paraphrases are comfortable with even more for the sake of even greater clarity. The problem, however, is that the responsibility of interpretation is not that of the translator but the reader. In an ideal world, the translators would give readers the pure "raw data" from the original language and the reader would make the judgment calls of interpretation based upon this data. Since this is not an ideal world, readers of translations simply need to be aware of this reality and read any translation with their eyes wide open.

Each of these categories has strengths and weaknesses. Since formal equivalence translations are relatively accurate with regard to the original languages, they make good study Bibles. They get the reader as close as possible to the original text without having to learn Hebrew and Greek. Use these as you are reflecting on the meaning and significance of words, phrases, and sentences of the biblical text. Their weakness is that they are rather clunky and choppy. They don't flow nicely; they are not reader-friendly. This is because they are more reflective of the Hebrew and Greek forms rather than the Standard English form.

The strength of dynamic or functional equivalence translations is that they do flow nicely, they sound good in English, and they are therefore more reader-friendly. Use these when you are reading the biblical text more devotionally, especially larger portions of it. Their weakness is that these translations contain more of the interpretation of the translators, and the reader is not always aware of when this is taking place.

This would also be a weakness of paraphrases. There is an even greater degree of interpretation for the sake of greater clarity in these. Therefore, these are not good Bibles to use for an in-depth study of the text. The strength of these versions is that they communicate the text of Scripture in a very fresh way. Personally, I find this helpful for texts of Scripture that I have heard or read many, many times. After a while, they can "go in one ear and out the other" without making much of an impact in between. This is not good! Paraphrases state these familiar texts in such a new way that it draws the reader back into the challenge of comprehension.

So which translation should you use? I think the best answer is to get good examples of all of these categories and use them appropriately. Read the foreword or preface of a translation. It will usually explain the philosophy of translation that is being followed. Translators want their readers to know this. Use a formal equivalence translation for going deep into a text of Scripture. Use a dynamic or functional equivalence translation for reading larger sections of Scripture. Use paraphrases to draw you back into the task of understanding and applying familiar texts of Scripture, or simply to hear God's Word in an innovative way.

FUN FACT

God has greatly blessed English speakers with many very good translations of the Bible. No other language even comes close in terms of available translations. We should be thankful for this, but also be good stewards of what God has given us by taking full advantage of these precious resources.

What Do We Mean
When We Say the Bible
Is the Word of God?

One of the most important reasons Christians believe that the Bible is the Word of God is because it makes that claim about itself. But that doesn't prove anything, does it? After all, other books, such as the Qur'an,[1] claim to have come from God.

But in the Bible's case, there is a lot of evidence to support what it says about itself, and in the next two chapters we will look at some of this evidence. Meanwhile, in this chapter we will explore what it means for us to say that the Bible is the Word of God.

The most straightforward claim about the Bible within the Bible itself is found in the first phrase of 2 Timothy 3:16: "All Scripture is God-breathed." Other versions, such as the New American Standard Bible, translate this verse, "All Scripture is inspired by God," making it one of the main verses that supports the Christian belief in the inspiration of Scripture, or the Bible. But the NIV translation is quite literal, as the Greek word precisely means "God-breathed." This word is only found here in the New Testament, so it is possible that Paul coined it to say what he wanted to say about the nature of Scripture.

The first implication of this word is that the Bible begins with God. He is the ultimate source of what is written in it. This word also contains the imagery of breathing out, which implies speaking or communicating. Therefore, the Bible finds its source in God and is the result of God's decision to communicate with people.

Another important text is 2 Peter 1:20–21, which speaks of the process God used to communicate his written Word. Verse 20 says, "Above all, you must understand that no prophecy of Scripture came about by the prophet's own interpretation of things." (The Greek word translated *interpretation* in the NIV is used only in the New Testament, and is therefore challenging to translate.) In light of the next verse, Peter rules out the idea that the prophets came up with the messages on their own: "For prophecy never had its origin in the human will, but prophets, though human, spoke from God as they were carried along by the Holy Spirit" (v. 21). The New English Translation has "No prophecy of Scripture ever comes about by the prophet's own *imagination*" (v. 20), and The New Living Translation puts it this way: "No prophecy in Scripture ever came from the prophet's *own understanding*, or from *human initiative*. No, those prophets were moved by the Holy Spirit, and they spoke from God" (vv. 20-21). The origin of Scripture is once again confirmed as God himself. Having decided to communicate, he did so through the Holy Spirit, the divine author of Scripture, who caused the human authors of the Bible to write what they wrote.

Based on these two important texts regarding the nature of the Bible (2 Timothy and 2 Peter), the Christian doctrine or teaching regarding the inspiration of the Bible can be summarized like this: God took the initiative to communicate to the people he had created. He did so through the work of the Holy Spirit, who empowered the human authors of Scripture. The result is that what the human authors wrote was in every sense the Word of God.

There is one drawback to referring to this great truth as *inspiration* because of the way we use words like *inspired, inspiring,* and *inspirational* in everyday life. It is common to hear someone mention how inspiring a pastor's sermon was, or how inspired a poet was when she wrote a touching poem, or how inspirational a Bach composition is. But what these comments imply is usually that the pastor, poet, or composer has produced a remarkable product that is very meaningful in some way. These are merely excellent *human* works of literature or art. Unfortunately, this meaning has also been attached to the idea of the inspiration of Scripture—it is only a great *human* piece of literature. The problem, however, is that this drains the supernatural dimension from the Bible.

This is not to deny the significance of the human authors and their ability and artistry. We should affirm what is called the "dual authorship" of Scripture—it is *both* a divine and a human book. Notice how these two aspects appear in the opening verses of Deuteronomy: "These are *the words Moses spoke* to all Israel. . . . Moses *proclaimed* to the Israelites all that *the* Lord *had commanded* him. . . . Moses *began to expound* this law, saying: 'The Lord *our God said* to us at Horeb. . .'" (Deuteronomy 1:1–6). Therefore, even though the Bible is genuinely a human book, the ultimate source and author is God himself.

Sometimes the inspiration of Scripture is mistakenly understood to mean that God simply dictated these words to the authors, reducing them to human word-processors. This is certainly true in a few cases, for example, the Ten Commandments and the other Old Testament laws. But for the most part, God worked through their intellects, experiences, and styles of expression in such a way that what they wrote was exactly what God intended.

There is mystery here in terms of how this worked; nevertheless, the Bible clearly implies that the very words the authors used were the exact words God chose for them to use. For example, God told the prophet Jeremiah, "Tell them everything I command you; do not omit a *word*" (Jeremiah 26:2). Later, Jeremiah himself declared, "The LORD has sent me to you to speak all these *words* in your hearing" (Jeremiah 26:15). God said to the prophet Ezekiel, "You must speak *my words* to them" (Ezekiel 2:7).

The New Testament expresses an equally high view of the Scriptures as God's words. When Jesus dealt with unbelieving Jewish leaders, he constantly did so based on the "Scriptures" (Matthew 21:42; 22:29). And in 1 Corinthians 2:13, Paul wrote, "This is what we speak, not in words taught us by human wisdom but in *words* taught by the Spirit." We also see that the New Testament writers also considered the books of the New Testament to be of the same nature as the books of the Old Testament (1 Timothy 5:18; 2 Peter 3:16) and equally authoritative (2 Thessalonians 3:14; 2 Peter 3:2).

So one reason we believe that the Bible is the Word of God is because it makes that claim for itself. This claim is validated by other evidence, which will be explored in the following chapters.

FUN FACT

Based on the Greek word in 2 Timothy 3:16, which literally means "God-breathed," maybe Christians should switch from using the word *inspiration* to *exhalation* to describe how God gave us the Bible.

What Internal Evidence Do We Have That the Bible Is the Word of God?

In the previous chapter, we looked at the two most important and explicit biblical texts regarding the nature of the Bible, and we concluded that the Bible is the very Word of God. In this chapter, we will look at evidence that supports this claim within the Bible itself.

Its unity. Even though the sixty-six different books of the Old and New Testaments were written by dozens of authors from different backgrounds, cultures, and levels of education, using three different languages over a period of more than 1,500 years, there is an amazing unity, continuity, and agreement throughout. What can explain this? That behind them all there is one source—God himself.

Fulfilled prophecy. In the Bible, there are many predictions of things that will happen in the future, and many of these predictions have already been fulfilled in very precise ways. These fall into the category of "internal evidence," because the Bible itself accurately records many of these fulfillments. But some can be categorized "external evidence," because many of these fulfillments can be confirmed by historical records outside the Bible. In the next chapter, we will provide some examples of fulfilled prophecies that have been documented outside of the Bible, but the following are some examples of prophecies that were fulfilled within the Scriptures, specifically concerning the coming of the Messiah, Jesus Christ.

Isaiah predicted, "The virgin will conceive and give birth to a son, and will call him Immanuel" (Isaiah 7:14). The fulfillment through the birth of Jesus to the Virgin Mary is recorded in Matthew 1:21–23, where Matthew quotes Isaiah 7:14.

There are also amazing prophecies in the book of Psalms, specifically in the category of messianic psalms. For example, Psalm 22 contains many anticipations of the crucifixion of Jesus. When he cried out, "My God, my God, why have you forsake me?" (Matthew 27:46) he was quoting Psalm 22:1. This psalm also predicts the mocking of Jesus (v. 7; Matthew 27:39-43), the piercing of his hands and feet (v. 16; John 20:25), and the casting of lots in order to divide his clothing (v. 18; John 19:23-24).

Micah 5:2 predicted that the future ruler of Israel, the Messiah, would be born in Bethlehem. This was fulfilled, as recorded in Matthew 2:1. In fact, when the Magi, or wise men, came to inquire as to where they could find the newborn king of the Jews, King Herod's advisors immediately referred to Micah 5:2 as the well-known prophecy of the birthplace of the Messiah (Matthew 2:4–6).

Jesus himself stated that the Old Testament prophets spoke of him and that what he did fulfilled those prophecies (Matthew 26:52–56; Luke 24:25–27, 44–45; John 5:39). Other New Testament writers acknowledged this. Matthew often quotes from the Old Testament and applies it to Jesus, as we saw above. John does this as well (John 19:36–37; 20:9).

There are hundreds of detailed prophecies throughout the Old Testament, all of which came true in Jesus Christ. How likely is it that so many such prophecies could be *coincidentally* fulfilled in a particular person in history? Peter W. Stone, in his book *Science Speaks*, examines the evidence.[1] Starting with the round figure of 300 prophecies of the first coming of Jesus, he determines the probability of just sixteen of those coincidentally being fulfilled in one individual: One in 10^{45}. To help us better understand this enormous number, he says that this is the number of silver dollars in a solid ball with its center at the earth and its radius thirty times the distance between the earth and the sun. The chance that someone could choose one marked silver dollar from that ball on the first try is the same chance of sixteen of the prophecies of Jesus' coming being fulfilled in one historical person. After computing the probability of this happening for forty-eight of the 300 prophecies (one in 10^{157}!), Stone concludes, "This is not merely evidence, it is proof of the Bible's inspiration by God—proof so definite that the universe is not large enough to hold the evidence."[2]

The resurrection of Jesus. This is one of many miracles recorded in the Bible, but it is also the most significant. If it could be proven that the historical, physical resurrection of Jesus never happened, the Bible would be thoroughly discredited. However, there is great evidence that Jesus was resurrected from the dead, exactly as Scripture claims he was. One piece of evidence is the willingness of his followers to die as witnesses of the living Jesus Christ, and almost all of them were, in fact, executed for this very reason. Would they have died for something that they knew was a lie, especially in significant numbers? It is very unlikely. Another piece of evidence is the inability of those who disputed the resurrection to produce the body of Jesus, which had been buried in a sealed tomb guarded by Roman soldiers. In addition, there were not only a few, but many eyewitnesses of Jesus after his resurrection.

What is truly amazing about the biblical record of the resurrection of Jesus is that, unlike any other religion or philosophy, Christianity makes itself vulnerable to being proven false. The Bible makes the *historical* claim that Jesus really came back from the dead, not just spiritually but physically. If historians could show beyond a reasonable doubt that this did not happen in history, not only would the Bible be discredited, but Christianity as a whole would crumble! (1 Corinthians 15:1–19). However, this will never happen because the resurrection is true, not only in abstract theory, but in objective history.

FUN FACT

Journalist Frank Morison set out to prove that the resurrection of Jesus never happened. As he did his research, he became convinced of the very opposite of what he had set out to demonstrate, and he was converted to Christianity. He wrote a book entitled *Who Moved the Stone?*[3] The first chapter is called "The Book That Refused to Be Written."

Is There External Evidence That the Bible Is the Word of God?

In the previous chapter, we looked at evidence within the Bible itself that it is the Word of God. In this chapter, we will consider evidence from outside of the Bible that supports this belief.

Fulfilled prophecy. The Bible contains many predictions of the future that were precisely fulfilled as documented by historical records outside of the Bible.

For example, in Daniel 9, we have the record of a brief but significant vision of the future, specifically a period of 490 years. Verse 25 says, "Know and understand this: From the time the word goes out to restore and rebuild Jerusalem until the Anointed One, the ruler, comes, there will be seven 'sevens,' and sixty-two 'sevens.'" The decree probably refers to one that was issued by the Persian King Artaxerxes in 445 or 444 BC. "Seven 'sevens' and sixty-two 'sevens'" adds up to 483 years. When adjustments are made for different calendars, the end of this period falls in the early AD 30s, at the end of the earthly life of Jesus, the "Anointed One" or Messiah, referred to in this verse. Verse 26 says that the Anointed One will be "put to death," the word referring to a violent death. This was fulfilled in the crucifixion of Jesus, an event referred to by at least two early extra-biblical sources, Josephus and Tacitus.

Daniel saw an amazingly detailed and extensive vision of the future as recorded in Daniel 11. Much of it was fulfilled in the next 400 years in what is called the intertestamental period. It includes references to Alexander the Great (v. 3) and how, when he died, his empire was divided up into four smaller kingdoms ruled by four of his generals (v. 4). Their successors and the effects they had on God's people and the land of Palestine are predicted and precisely fulfilled.

What can explain the precise and detailed fulfillment of these and many other prophecies in the Bible? They can only be explained as being revealed to the prophets by God, from whom history flows as the outworking of his plans.

Archaeological findings. If the Bible is the Word of God, it is to be expected that the history recorded therein is accurate. However, there have been occasions when scholars have claimed that some historical records in the Bible are inaccurate. In some of these cases, archaeology has overturned these claims and demonstrated the accuracy of biblical history. For example, critics of the Bible had claimed that, contrary to Daniel 5, there was no King Belshazzar who reigned during the Babylonian Empire in the sixth century BC. However, the discovery of the Nabonidus Cylinder in southern Iraq in the mid-1850s identified Belshazzar as the son of King Nabonidus, who co-reigned with his father from around 553 to 539 BC. In 539 BC, their empire fell to the Persians, confirming what is recorded in Daniel 5:22–30.

Similarly, critics claimed that the Hittites never existed, even though they are often mentioned in the Old Testament. But again, archaeological findings in 1906, including the discovery of the Hittites' ancient capital city, Hattusa, confirmed their existence. In fact, the treaty form used by the Hittites is also the form reflected in the covenant that God made with the new nation of Israel after the exodus, known as the Mosaic or Sinai covenant. (This will be discussed further in chapter 29.)

Preservation and quantity of biblical manuscripts. None of the original documents written by the authors of Scripture have survived to this day, but there are many copies or manuscripts of those documents. The discovery of the Dead Sea Scrolls, in 1947, many of which were copies of Old Testament books (in fact, the only Old Testament book not found among them was Esther), confirmed how accurately these books have been copied and preserved in the many centuries since they were written.

The number of surviving manuscripts of the books of the New Testament is astounding. There are nearly 6,000 copies of all or parts of the Greek New Testament, and more are being discovered all the time. Other ancient literature can only claim as few as around twenty copies, or in a few rare cases, up to 200. Also, the time span between some of the original New Testament documents and the earliest remaining copies averages around 300 years. The Saint John Fragment, a copy of John 18:31–33 on the one side and John 18:37–38 on the other side, is dated around thirty years after the original was written! For other ancient literature, the time span is often between 400 and 700 years, or more.

What could explain the vast number of biblical manuscripts, especially for the New Testament, and how well they have been preserved and accurately copied as compared to manuscripts of other ancient literature? The answer is that God supernaturally preserves his Word.

Worldwide influence. The Bible has been influential in every time period and in every culture to which it has been taken. The publishing facts alone confirm this. It is by far the bestselling publication of all time. The Bible was the first book to be printed by Johannes Gutenberg. The Bible has been translated into more languages and read by more people than any other book.

Transformed lives. As a result of its circulation, the Bible has transformed more lives than any other book in history. This is a subjective element to be sure, but it must be taken into account. Millions of people through the centuries would affirm that the Bible has proven itself worthy in their own lives through its encouragement, assurance, challenge, and confrontation. This is especially significant in terms of individuals who were once skeptics with regard to the Bible and Christianity, such as atheists (e.g., C. S. Lewis), journalists (Frank Morison, Lee Strobel), scientists (e.g., Alister McGrath), scholars (e.g., Sir William Ramsey), intellectuals (e.g., Aleksandr Solzhenitsyn), Marxists (e.g., Marvin Olasky), and adherents of other religions (many recent converts from Islam). Once these people were exposed to the teachings of the Bible, their lives were changed forever.

These are a few of the lines of evidence from outside the Bible that indicate the Bible is indeed God's Word.

FUN FACT

One of the more remarkable prophecies in the Bible is found in Isaiah 44:28 and 45:1, 13. An individual whom God would work through to restore the city of Jerusalem is referred to *by name*—Cyrus. This clearly refers to Cyrus the Great, the first king of the Persian Empire, who reigned from 559-530 BC. Isaiah refers to him by name nearly 150 years before he lived!

Why Does It Matter That the Bible Is the Word of God?

If the Bible is, in fact, the Word of God, then there are some important things we need to consider. Scripture itself tells us some of these things.

The Bible is true. God is always truthful and correct in everything he says (2 Samuel 7:28; Titus 1:2; Hebrews 6:18), therefore his Word is also truthful and correct in whatever it says (Psalm 12:6; Proverbs 30:5). Jesus said to his Father, "Your word is truth" (John 17:17). He does not merely say God's Word is true, but he equates it with truth itself—ultimate Truth. This means that the Bible is inerrant, or without error. This certainly applies to spiritual matters, but must also apply to every other kind of matter, whether scientific, historical (more on this in chapter 29), or anything else.

Jesus' own understanding of this can be seen in John 10. Jesus claimed deity for himself by saying, "I and the Father are one" (v. 30). The Jews' response was to pick up stones to execute him for blasphemy. Jesus then said, "Is it not written in your Law, 'I have said you are "gods"'? If he called them 'gods,' to whom the word of God came—and the Scripture cannot be set aside—what about the one whom the Father set apart as his very own and sent into the world? Why then do you accuse me of blasphemy because I said, 'I am God's Son'?" (vv. 34–36). Jesus believed that the Scriptures "cannot be set aside," that is, they cannot be shown to be false or wrong in any way (NIV 1984 says, "cannot be broken"). Furthermore, he backs up this claim on the basis of one word—*gods* (*elohim*)—in the middle of one verse from the psalms—Psalm 82:6.[1] What is even more amazing is that he was staking his own life on one word from one verse in the Hebrew Scriptures! To Jesus, every word of Scripture is perfect.

The Bible is trustworthy. Because God is faithful and can be trusted to do what he says (Numbers 23:19; 1 Corinthians 1:9; 1 Thessalonians 5:24), the Bible, as the Word of God, can also be trusted (2 Samuel 7:28). This is what the term *infallibility* means. It is often used as a synonym for *inerrancy,* but, to be precise, it takes it one step further: Because the Bible is without error, it will never fail in its message or purpose, nor will it ever cause anyone to fail or lead them into error, or fool them into believing something that is not worthy of belief.

An amazing statement of Jesus that reflects this idea is found in Matthew 5:17–18: "Do not think that I have come to abolish the Law or the Prophets; I have not come to abolish them but to fulfill them. For truly I tell you, until heaven and earth disappear, not the smallest letter, not the least stroke of a pen, will by any means disappear from the Law until everything is accomplished." When Jesus referred to the "Law or the Prophets," he had in mind all of the Scriptures of that time—the Hebrew Scriptures, or what we call the Old Testament. His assertion, then, was that from those Scriptures, not the smallest letter or least pen stroke would be lost until the end of time. The smallest letter in the language that Jesus spoke was a *yodh,* or a Y. It would look to us like an apostrophe

(') written at the top of a line of letters with just the flick of the wrist. The "least pen stroke" referred to a part of a letter that distinguishes it from another letter. If we start with a *P* and add a stroke at the bottom, we end up with an *R*. If we start with an *I* and add a stroke at the top, we have a *T*. So the amazing thing that Jesus is saying is that until the end of time, God will protect and preserve his written Word down to individual words, letters, and even parts of letters! He would not do this unless it were all true and trustworthy (see also Matthew 24:35).

The Bible is a unity. Because the Bible ultimately comes from one mind, namely God's, it reflects a perfect harmony of thought. Therefore, there are no contradictions in the Bible, just as there are no contradictions in God's mind. Every biblical text complements and agrees with all other biblical texts. This is not to deny that the Bible will sometimes *seem* to contradict itself, but we will take this matter up in another chapter.

The Bible is authoritative. Because God is our ultimate authority, the Bible is our ultimate, written authority. This means that its authority comes from God, not from any human source. Therefore, its authority is greater than any human (pastor, priest, bishop, king, president, prime minister), human institution (church, denomination, council, senate, parliament, court), or human document (creed, catechism, confession, doctrinal statement, ordinance, law). This also means that, like God, the Bible deserves to be believed and obeyed. To disbelieve it or to disobey it is to disbelieve or disobey God himself.

This is why the Old Testament prophets continually called the nation of Israel to obey the law of God contained in the Hebrew Scriptures. At the very end of the Old Testament, God said through his prophet Malachi, "Remember the law of my servant Moses, the decrees and laws I gave him at Horeb for all Israel" (Malachi 4:4). This is what Paul meant when he wrote, "What I am writing to you is the Lord's command" (1 Corinthians 14:37).

If the Bible is the Word of God, then. . . . We could go on and on. There are many implications of this amazing truth. We have looked at only some of the more important ones.

FUN FACT

God's words are inherently authoritative. This seems to be what people recognized in the teaching of Jesus, as Matthew notes at the end of the Sermon on the Mount: "The crowds were amazed at his teaching, because he taught as one who had authority, and not as their teachers of the law" (Matthew 7:28-29).

Is All the History in the Bible Accurate?

There have been many claims over the years that the historical records found in the Bible are inaccurate. Sometimes people make these claims simply because they don't believe in the supernatural realm—or if they do, they don't think that realm ever intersects with the natural realm. Obviously, this belief would rule out God's working in history, especially when it comes to the historical events recorded in the Bible that involve miracles (for example, the parting of the Red Sea and the resurrection of Jesus). But if we believe in a God who can and does work in history, then historical events that involve miracles would not be a problem. Neither belief system can be absolutely proven, but we must at least acknowledge our beliefs and make sure they are valid.

The more specific claims regarding inaccuracies in biblical history have been thoroughly examined by many and found to be unconvincing. In earlier chapters, we looked at a few examples of how archaeology has shown biblical history to be accurate, and since history and archaeology are so closely tied together, let us consider a few more examples.

A common claim of critics is that the Old Testament patriarchs, including Moses, could not have lived as long ago as the Bible suggests. However, documents found at ancient sites, such as Nuzi, or Nuzu, in present-day Iraq, and Mari in present-day Syria, have revealed a culture very similar to that of the patriarchs that dates back to the time the Bible claims they lived. For example, the practice of having a household maid bear a child in the place of a barren wife is documented in ancient texts, just as Abraham and Sarai accomplished through Hagar and her son, Ishmael (Genesis 16). Laws regarding the selling of one's birthright to a brother have also been found, just as Esau did to Jacob (Genesis 25:27–35). Excavations in the southern part of Israel (Negev), where the patriarchs spent much of their time, also verify biblical chronology and show that this area was inhabited during the time of the patriarchs by people who practiced agriculture, just as the patriarchs did.

Critics have also claimed that codes of laws did not come into existence until after the time that the Bible says Moses lived. However, archaeologists have since discovered that such legal systems existed well before the time of Moses, the best-known example being the Code of Hammurabi. Findings from Ugarit, in present-day Syria, have revealed religious practices (sacrifices, priests, temples) that are very similar to those prescribed in the Old Testament Law. Archaeologists have also confirmed the biblical record that when Israel invaded Canaan under Joshua, the only cities destroyed by fire were Jericho (Joshua 6:24), Ai (Joshua 8:28), and Hazor (Joshua 11:11–13). In 2007, Dr. Eilat Mazar, an Israeli archaeologist, announced that she had discovered a part of Nehemiah's wall, dating to the sixth to fifth centuries BC, confirming the facts and date of Nehemiah 1–6. These are just a few of the examples of archaeology not only confirming Old Testament history, but helping us better understand this history in its historical and cultural setting.

Recently, there has been much criticism of the historical accuracy of the New Testament Gospels and the book of Acts. In response, we need to remember the huge number of New Testament manuscripts and how close they are to the original documents, as we discussed in a previous chapter. This would argue for the faithful preservation of the historical data in these documents. But the question remains: were they historically accurate in the first place? We must note, again, that the New Testament writers would have wanted to be accurate for the sake of biblical morality and the integrity of the gospel message. John wrote about himself as an eyewitness of many of the events he recorded: "The man who saw it has given testimony, and his testimony is true. He knows that he tells the truth, and he testifies so that you also may believe" (John 19:35; see also what Luke, who was not an eyewitness, wrote: Luke 1:1–4).

But even if they had wanted to be accurate, that doesn't necessarily mean they were able to be accurate. After all, the earliest gospels were not written until twenty to thirty years after Jesus' ascended into heaven. These true stories would have been passed along verbally, but as the old game of "telephone" demonstrates, a message gets distorted as it is passed along from person to person. This might be all the more true over two or three decades. But as historians have shown, the ancients had amazing abilities to memorize information and remember it accurately. They had to be able to do this, since they did not have an easy way to record information. In addition, when the Gospels were written, there were still enough living eyewitnesses to the life of Jesus that would have detected and corrected mistakes or lies in the accounts. In this sense, the game of "telephone" is not a valid analogy, because the stories of Jesus were not whispered from ear to ear but rather proclaimed publicly to many people, many of whom could have pointed out inaccuracies if they existed.

Luke particularly has been both attacked and vindicated with regard to its history. Archaeologists have shown Luke to be particularly accurate with regard to government titles, for example, "proconsul" (Acts 13:7; 18:12), "politarchs" (Acts 17:6, 8; translated in the NIV as "city officials"), and the Greek term *strategoi* for the city officials in the Roman colony of Philippi (Acts 16:20, 22ff.; translated in the NIV as "magistrates"). All of these have been shown to be the exact titles that were appropriate in each situation. Luke has also been shown to be very precise in matters of chronology and geography.

We should not conclude that all challenges regarding the historicity of the Bible have been answered yet. But many claims of historical inaccuracies in Scripture have been proven wrong by further historical research, and none of these claims has been proven to be actual inaccuracies. In other words, we have good reasons to assume that biblical history is accurate and reliable and that further research will continue to verify this.

FUN FACT

Sir William Ramsey (1851–1939) was an eminent British archaeologist who believed that the book of Acts was written in mid-second century AD rather than the mid-first century, and whoever wrote it had made quite a few historical blunders. But as a result of his own research, he became convinced not only that Acts was written in the first century, but that Luke, the author, was a very accurate and trustworthy historian. His research and conclusions were published in his books *The Bearing of Recent Discovery on the Trustworthiness of the New Testament*[1] and *St. Paul the Traveler and the Roman Citizen.*[2] A skeptic was turned into a believer.

Why Is the
Bible Sometimes
Confusing?

Anybody who has ever read the Bible has struggled with parts that have confused them. This should not surprise us, but rather we should expect it for a number of reasons. But before we look at these, we should note that Christians also believe in what has been called the clarity of Scripture. This means that the most important concepts in Scripture are clear and understandable to those who read it in dependence upon God and who humbly desire to understand it, believe it, and follow it. Psalm 19:7 says, "The statutes of the LORD are trustworthy, making wise the simple" (see also Psalm 119:130). So even though there may be some things in Scripture that are confusing, the parts that are vital to understand can be readily understood by God's design.

The first reason the Bible can sometimes be confusing is because it is the record of God's thoughts and ways. As we read it, we are trying to better understand God himself. The problem is that our finite human minds are ultimately unable to understand the infinite thoughts and ways of God. God himself says, "For my thoughts are not your thoughts, neither are your ways my ways. . . . As the heavens are higher than the earth, so are my ways higher than your ways and my thoughts than your thoughts" (Isaiah 55:8–9). This is further complicated by God's holiness and perfection, especially as we compare it to the sinfulness of our human minds. Jeremiah 17:9 says, "The heart is deceitful above all things and beyond cure. Who can understand it?" The Old Testament concept of the heart includes the immaterial things that are going on within us—thoughts, attitudes, motives, desires. Scripture is clear that sin has twisted and distorted the human mind. So this, too, greatly complicates our understanding of the things of God found in his Word. This should make us humble as we come to the Bible, leading us to depend on God himself for the help we need to overcome these handicaps.

Another reason related to this, but in itself hard to understand, is that God intended his Word to be confusing to those who did not want to know and believe it in the first place. Jesus told his disciples that he often spoke in parables or stories to both reveal *and* conceal the truth. He said, "The knowledge of the secrets of the kingdom of heaven has been given to you, but not to them. Whoever has will be given more, and they will have an abundance. Whoever does not have, even what they have will be taken from them. This is why I speak to them in parables: 'Though seeing, they do not see; though hearing, they do not hear or understand'" (Matthew 13:11–13, quoting from Jeremiah 5:21). He goes on to quote from Isaiah 6:9–10. Therefore, this principle was also in effect in the Old Testament through God's messengers, the prophets. The point is that there are things God wants to reveal *only* to those who already believe in him and are sincerely looking for truth. But for those who are not, parts of the Bible are divinely intended to be confusing. Paul puts it this way: "The person without the Spirit does not accept the things that come from the Spirit of God but considers them foolishness, and cannot understand them because they are discerned only through the Spirit" (1 Corinthians 2:14). The very important implication is this: To understand the Bible, one must have faith in God and a genuine desire to understand what God has revealed. God will reward this by opening our eyes with the gift of understanding.

A third reason the Bible may be confusing is because life itself is complicated and confusing. A part of what God provides for us through the Bible is an *explanation* of the world around us and life as we experience it as well as *solutions* to the many problems found in the world and life. We live in a complicated world to begin with (for example, do you understand string theory?) and sin has made it even more complicated. All of this makes for challenging depictions of the nature of reality and complex solutions to the problems created by sin. The ultimate solution to these problems is Christ and his death and resurrection, but even the Bible acknowledges that this is foolishness to unbelievers (1 Corinthians 1:18). Again, the answer is to believe: "God was pleased through the foolishness of what was preached to save those who believe" (1 Corinthians 1:21).

A fourth reason the Bible is confusing is because even though God intended it for all people of all times and places, it was originally written to certain peoples in certain cultural settings in certain historical periods. The Old Testament contains many references to farming, animals, crops, and plants that the intended audience would understand through personal experience, but for twenty-first-century city-dwellers, these references are puzzling. The New Testament epistles contain references to master-slave relationships (e.g., Ephesians 6:5–9) and "food sacrificed to idols"

(1 Corinthians 8:1). These address common situations in the Roman Empire in the first century AD, but again, are baffling to the modern reader. So our challenge today is to try to crawl into the minds and experiences of the original audience so that we can understand Scripture the way they would have understood it. Only then can we better understand how it applies to us thousands of years later (and it does!).

Another possible reason for the Bible being sometimes hard to understand is that this is a God-intended means of continually drawing us back to Scripture in order to wrestle with it. Think about it: If God were easy to understand, he would not be worth worshiping; if God's Word were easy to understand, it would not be worth studying. How often are we drawn back to children's books to read and reread them so that we can understand them better and benefit from their great wisdom? There are riches to be found in the Word of God. And as is true of most kinds of riches, they are not obtained easily, but they are worth the hard work. David said that the law, statutes, precepts, and commands of God "are more precious than gold, than much pure gold; they are sweeter than honey, than honey from the honeycomb. By them your servant is warned; in keeping them there is great reward" (Psalm 19:7–11). If we long for the greatest kinds of riches—those that come from God—we will continually be engaged with Scripture, despite the challenges and hard work that entails.

All of these reasons should motivate us not only to *read* but also to *study* the Bible. God is an infinite and holy God, and we are challenged to understand him with finite and fallen minds. The Bible discusses difficult problems and presents difficult solutions, and we are challenged to comprehend both. The Bible was written to people long ago in very different settings, and we are challenged to understand things now that they understood intuitively then. How can we do that? That is the topic of chapter 32.

COMFORTING FACT

Even the apostle Peter admitted that some of what the apostle Paul wrote was confusing: "[Our dear brother Paul] writes the same way in all his letters, speaking in them of these matters. *His letters contain some things that are hard to understand* " (2 Peter 3:16). That should make the rest of us feel better.

How Do I Reconcile the Fact That the Bible Seems to Contradict Itself?

This really is a more specific form of the question "Why is the Bible so confusing?" God is God and we are not. His thoughts and ways are higher than ours. We are trying to understand his Word with very small and very depraved minds, so it should not surprise us that there *seem* to be contradictions in Scripture; rather, we should expect it. It is part of the exciting challenge of understanding the Bible.

There is a long history of claims that there are contradictions in the Bible. But it is important to note that none of these claims has been proven very convincing over time. This is not to say that all apparent contradictions have been clearly and unambiguously shown not to be contradictions at all. But it is safe to say that all claims of contradictions have been thoroughly examined and satisfactory explanations have been offered.

One classic example of a possible contradiction is what the apostle James wrote as compared to what the apostle Paul wrote. Numerous times, Paul vigorously argued that one is "justified" or made right with God by faith apart from works or anything that we do. For example, in Ephesians 2:8–9, he says, "For it is by grace you have been saved, through faith—and this is not from yourselves, it is the gift of God—not by works, so that no one can boast." But James writes: "You see that a person is considered righteous by what they do and not by faith alone" (James 2:24). At first glance, this seems to be a blatant contradiction. Paul says that we are justified by faith and not works. James says that we are justified by works in addition to faith.

In light of situations such as this, we need to remember something about the nature of the Bible that we have already discussed: its unity. This principle says that if God is the ultimate author of Scripture, and if God does not contradict himself (his thoughts are perfect), nor does he deceive anyone (he is a God of integrity and truthfulness), then no contradictions will be found in the written Word of God. Neither will any human author of Scripture contradict any other human author of Scripture because God, through the Holy Spirit, guided all of them to write what they wrote. This, however, does not rule out *apparent* contradictions. These are called paradoxes, things that seem to be contradictory but are not.

An important principle for interpreting the Bible, called "the analogy of faith," is that we should use Scripture to interpret Scripture. By this method, we use clearer Scriptures to help explain more ambiguous Scriptures, such as apparent contradictions. So if we apply this principle to the issue between Paul and James, we will discover that the clear and consistent teaching of Scripture is that an individual is saved or "justified before God" by faith or belief alone. Paul says this over and over again through his letters (e.g., Romans 3:20–28; 5:1; Galatians 2:16; 3:11). Other New Testament authors would agree (see John 1:12; 3:15–18; Acts 16:30–31). Theologically, the concept of grace would rule out anything that we might do to "deserve" or "earn" salvation; grace and works are mutually exclusive ideas (Galatians 5:4). So Scripture is clear that salvation is indeed by faith alone apart from works.

So is James wrong? Does he contradict Paul and other biblical writers? On closer examination, the answer to both of these questions becomes apparent—no. The broader context of what James wrote (James 2:14–26) indicates that he had a different concern in mind than Paul did, namely, he is writing to Christians who think that since salvation is by grace and received by faith alone, they can live any way they want to. James, then, is writing to show that the kind of faith that results in salvation (see chapter 2) demonstrates that it is genuine, gives evidence that it is true faith. This is the nature of the works that James says must accompany faith. They are not good works in order for one *to be* saved, but rather good works that a Christian does because he or she *has been* saved. His two examples show this: Abraham believed God (James 2:23, which quotes Genesis 15:6) and then demonstrated the genuineness of his faith when he was willing to sacrifice his son, Isaac (James 2:21–22, alluding to Genesis 22:1–14). Rahab believed God, and then she protected the spies of Israel (James 2:25).

James would agree with Paul that salvation is by faith alone apart from works. He just takes an additional step to clarify that the kind of faith that saves also shows itself through good works. And Paul would agree with James about that. Read Titus 3:4–8 to see how Paul makes both of these important points in one context: "He saved us, not because of righteous things we had done . . . having been justified by his grace . . . so that those who have trusted in God may be careful to devote themselves to doing what is good."

So what do you do when the Bible seems to contradict itself? First, trust that this is indeed only an apparent contradiction—not a real contradiction. Second, realize that apparent contradictions are often simply misinterpretations of Scripture. So again, we should be motivated to interpret Scripture correctly. The next chapter addresses this important topic.

FUN FACT

Even a theological giant like Martin Luther believed that James was contradicting Paul and Luther's beloved (and correct!) doctrine of justification by faith alone. As a result, he did not think the book of James deserved to be in the New Testament canon. He called James an "epistle of straw," that is, not worth much! Even theological giants don't understand everything perfectly.

What Do I Do
When I Don't Understand
What I'm Reading?

As we saw in the previous two chapters, the Bible can some-times be confusing or sound contradictory. Nevertheless, there are great riches of wisdom to be found in it, which should motivate us to understand it. Second Timothy 2:15 says, "Do your best to present yourself to God as one approved, a worker who does not need to be ashamed and who correctly handles the word of truth." Even though most of us are not pastors like Timothy was, what Paul told him applies to all of us. God's Word is true and precious, and therefore it deserves to be handled correctly. But how do we do that?

This chapter is an introduction to a simple but helpful approach to studying the Bible that can produce great results. There are three steps to this method: observation, interpretation, and application.[1] The observation step is where you try to answer the question "What is there to see?" In the interpretation step you ask, "What does it mean?" And finally, in the application step, you try to figure out what difference it makes.

Observation. Most of us wrongly assume that after reading something once, we know what it says. In reality, this isn't usually the case. Most Bible scholars agree that we must read a particular passage numerous times before we really begin to see what is there to be seen. In other words, the task of observation is not something that is accomplished easily. We have to read a passage over and over again and look hard for what is there. Think about one of those "Can you find it?" drawings where there are ten objects "hidden" in plain sight. Even though you are looking right at them from the outset, you have to look long and hard to distinguish all ten. That is how Scripture is. There is much to be seen immediately and obviously. Much more can be seen only after looking again and again at the text.

Some of the questions that we need to keep in mind as we observe a passage are as follows: "What are the important words being used?" "What is the genre or literary category of the material—narrative, history, poetry, prophecy?" "What other literary forms are being used—comparison, contrast, question-answer, cause-effect, repetition, emphasis, conditions (if, then)?" "Who is the author and what is known about him?" "Who was the original audience?" "What is the author's argument or flow of thought?" "Why is the author writing this?" If you are reading a narrative or a story, ask these kinds of questions: "Who are the characters?" "Where and when does this take place?" As you read and reread the passage with these questions in mind, write down what you think are the answers along with other thoughts and observations.

Interpretation. The goal here is to understand the passage you're reading as the original audience was intended to understand it. Or to put it in the form of a question, "What did the original author intend to communicate to his original readers?" In the interpretation stage, you should try to verify or modify the tentative answers to the questions that were asked in the observation step.

There are three broad principles of interpretation. First, interpret the text historically. This involves learning everything you can about the time, culture, geography, authors, and audiences of the original setting. This would also include determining the reason and purpose of the text. Why was it written? What did the author hope to accomplish?

Second, with regard to prose (as opposed to poetry) interpret the text grammatically. Try to understand how the passage is structured. What are the important parts of speech—verbs, nouns, pronouns, modifiers, connectives (small, but very important)? How are the sentences ordered? What are the paragraphs or blocks of thought (don't assume paragraph divisions in English Bibles are best)? What is the author's flow-of-thought or logic in the passage?

Third, and perhaps most important, interpret the passage contextually. What does a certain word mean within its sentence (most words have multiple meanings depending on their context)? What does a sentence mean within its paragraph? What does a paragraph mean within its chapter? The reason this is so important is because the meaning of the building blocks of literature (words, sentences, paragraphs) is determined by their context.

Much more could and should be said regarding interpretation, but let me just add that there are many very excellent resources available to help with this step: study Bibles, Bible dictionaries, encyclopedias, Bible handbooks, commentaries, and more. Take advantage of these.

Application. Although the authors of Scripture were writing for specific people in specific situations, God also intended what they wrote to be for all people of all times and places. So the question to be answered here is "How does this passage apply to me/us now?" This involves three steps: First, identify specific and concrete applications to the original audience. Second, identify the general and more abstract applications that are timeless, universal principles for all people of all times. A good example is the way Jesus showed the general principles behind the Old Testament law when he said, "'Love the Lord your God with all your heart and with all your soul and with all your mind.' This is the first and greatest commandment. And the second is like it: 'Love your neighbor as yourself.' All the Law and the Prophets hang on these two commandments" (Matthew 22:37–40). Third, identify specific concrete applications for yourself in your own twenty-first-century situation. To use Jesus' words as an example, questions of application might be: "What can I do to better love God with my heart? My soul? My mind?" "What can I do to better love others as I love myself?" The more specific and concrete the better the application.

God intended that his Word not only convey important information but also accomplish individual transformation. This cannot happen apart from thoughtful, personal application of Scripture.

ASSURING FACT

We are not left on our own when studying the Bible. Jesus promised that the Holy Spirit would guide us into all truth (John 14:26; 16:13; see also 1 Corinthians 2:12-14). We need to foster a healthy dependence upon the Spirit of God as we seek to truly understand what the Bible has to say.

What Does the Bible Tell Us About What God Is Like?

If you read the entire Bible and categorized every remark about the nature of God, most of the descriptions would regard his overall greatness, power, majesty, authority, reign, or dominion over *everything*. This is what theologians call the sovereignty of God. You can see this throughout the creation account in the amazing power God has to make things happen just by speaking; things that didn't exist came into being just because he said so (Genesis 1; Psalm 33:6, 9). But to take it one step further, because God is the creator of all things, he also owns all things (Deuteronomy 10:14; Psalm 24:1). And because he is the creator of all things, he has authority over all things—in other words, he has the right to rule (Psalm 47:2). He is the "God of gods and Lord of lords" (Deuteronomy 10:17). The title *Adonai* reflects the sovereignty of

God. It appears first in Genesis 15:2, where Abraham refers to God as "Sovereign LORD" (*Adonai Yahweh*), and nearly 300 times in the rest of the Old Testament.

The prayers in the Bible are filled with references to the sovereignty of God. Read David's prayer in 1 Chronicles 29:10–16; God's sovereignty permeates these verses. Similarly, Nehemiah begins his prayer by saying, "You alone are the LORD. You made the heavens, even the highest heavens, and all their starry host, the earth and all that is on it, the seas and all that is in them. You give life to everything, and the multitudes of heaven worship you" (9:6). The earliest Christians prayed in the same way: "They raised their voices together in prayer to God. 'Sovereign Lord,' they said, 'you made the heavens and the earth and the sea, and everything in them'" (Acts 4:24). Even Christians who were martyred due to their faith in Christ acknowledged the sovereignty of God in their prayers (Revelation 6:10).

The sovereignty of God also implies other aspects of his nature. For example, he is all-powerful (Jeremiah 32:17, 27), all-knowing (Isaiah 40:13–14), totally self-sufficient (Acts 17:24–25), and totally free to do whatever pleases him (Psalm 115:3). If he were not all these things, he would not be sovereign over *all things*. So the predominant characteristic of God that leaps from nearly every page of Scripture is his sovereignty.

But in addition to sovereignty, the Bible teaches us other characteristics of God, although some of these can be hard to fit together. On the one hand, God is said to be holy (Leviticus 11:44; Isaiah 6:3) and righteous or "just" (Genesis 18:25; Psalm 51:4). These words mean that God is morally perfect—he always does what is good and right—and therefore he holds everyone accountable for their own moral choices. He punishes the wicked and blesses the righteous. On the other hand, God is said to be a God of love (1 John 4:8, 16), mercy (Exodus 33:19; Romans 9:15–18), and grace (Psalm 103:8; Romans 3:24; Titus 2:11). God is love because he desires the very best for the objects of his love. God is merciful in that he does *not* give people what they *do* deserve, namely, punishment for sin. God is gracious in that he *does* give people what they do *not* deserve, namely, his goodness and blessing.

But if God is merciful, why would he condemn anyone for their sin? If God is loving, how could he send anyone to hell? If God is just, and we are all sinners (Romans 3:23), how can anyone be saved? These are not easy questions to answer, but we need to acknowledge that the writers of Scripture do not see these as contradictory. Instead, they keep these aspects of God's nature in careful balance and harmony, often in the very same contexts. For example, God himself says, "For a brief moment I abandoned you, but with deep compassion I will bring you back. In a surge of anger I hid my face from you for a moment, but with everlasting kindness I will have compassion on you" (Isaiah 54:7–8). Notice the movement from judgment to salvation, to judgment, to salvation. In Ezekiel 18, God calls his people to repentance, and if they do not repent, he threatens judgment: "The one who sins is the one who will die. The child will not share the guilt of the parent, nor will the parent share the guilt of the child. The righteousness of the righteous will be credited to them, and the wickedness of the wicked will be charged against them" (v. 20). This shows the justice or righteousness of God. But God goes on to say, "But if a wicked person turns away from all the sins they have committed and keeps all my decrees and does what is just and right, that person will surely live; they will not die. None of the offenses they have committed will be remembered against them. Because of the righteous things they have done, they will live. Do I take any pleasure in the death of the wicked? declares the Sovereign Lord. Rather, am I not pleased when they turn from their ways and live?" (vv. 21–23). This shows God's heart of compassion and his longing to forgive. We see the balance between God's justice and God's mercy in verses 30–32.

Even though it may not be clear to us how these aspects of God's nature fit together, we can be confident they do. No characteristic of God ever contradicts another characteristic of God; all the aspects of his nature are complementary to all other aspects. Therefore, we must work hard to keep our understanding of God in biblical balance. This is serious business, because many Christians down through the centuries have tended to emphasize one side of God's characteristics almost to the exclusion of the other side. For example, if the love and grace of God are emphasized over his holiness and justice, it can lead to believing in Universalism—everyone is going to end up in heaven and no one in hell. On the other hand, if the holiness and justice of God are emphasized over his compassion and mercy, it can lead to legalism—obey God's rules or face his punishment. Neither of these extremes represents the perfect balance within the character of God.

Much more could and should be said about the nature of God, but suffice it to say that God, as presented in the Bible, is a great God, who is worthy of adoration and worship as he really is, not only how we would like him to be. Therefore, he ought to be desired and sought above all else (Jeremiah 9:23–24).

GREAT FACT

When you accept God as he is described in Scripture and trust in him, you will never be disappointed. Rather, you will find him to be all-satisfying, the greatest treasure to be enjoyed (Psalm 37:4).

Where in the Bible Can I Find the Comfort That God Cares for Me?

God is very big, and we are very small. Is it reasonable to think that God cares for us as humans, let alone for each of us as individuals? David wondered about this in Psalm 8. After reflecting on the majesty and glory of God in verses 1–2, he asks, "When I consider your heavens, the work of your fingers . . . what is mankind that you are mindful of them, human beings that you care for them?" (vv. 3–4). Even though it is mind-boggling that the God of the universe would pay any attention to the situations and needs of any of us, the Bible is clear that indeed he does, and intimately so.

One reason for God's care for us comes from what David immediately goes on to say in Psalm 8: "You have made them [humans] a little lower than the angels and crowned them with glory and honor" (v. 5). This reflects the fact that God created humans to bear his image (Genesis 1:27) and to be in a personal relationship with him. As such, he cares about us as the pinnacle of his created order; he cares for those he created to be in a relationship with him.

The apostle Peter clearly states God's care in 1 Peter 5:7, "Cast all your anxiety on him because he cares for you," so there should be no doubt that God cares for us as humans generally (the "you" in this verse is plural). But the question remains: Does he care for us specifically as individuals? Does he care for *me*? Again, the biblical answer is clear and repeated—yes! Consider some of the evidence.

In Psalm 139, David makes amazing statements about God's knowledge of David himself as an individual: "You have searched me, LORD, and you know me. You know when I sit and when I rise; you perceive my thoughts from afar. You discern my going out and my lying down; you are familiar with all my ways. Before a word is on my tongue you, LORD, know it completely" (vv. 1–4). It would seem that if God did *not* care *for* me, he wouldn't care *about* me. But just the opposite is true. These verses describe an intimate, thorough, divine knowledge of an individual. It follows, then, that because God cares to know so much about the person, he will care profoundly for the person.

Another indicator that God cares for us as individuals is the very concept of prayer. God created us to be in relationship with him, and as everyone knows, good communication is vital for a good relationship. Because that is what God wants with us, he gave us the gift of prayer as a means of communicating with him for the sake of a healthy relationship with him. Any prayer in the Bible would illustrate this, but David is an especially great example throughout the psalms, many of which are prayers to God. For example, he says, "Have mercy on *me*, LORD, for I am faint" (Psalm 6:2), and "Turn, LORD, and deliver *me;* save *me* because of your unfailing love" (Psalm 6:4). The assumption that undergirds the very concept of prayer is that it is a God-given means of person-to-person communication.

Jesus spoke of the depth of God's care for individuals when he said, "Are not two sparrows sold for a penny? Yet not one of them will fall to the ground outside your Father's care. And even the very hairs of your head are all numbered. So don't be afraid; you are worth more than many sparrows" (Matthew 10:29–31; see also Matthew 6:29). The practical application of this is for us to trust God more and be less anxious. Jesus said, "Do not worry about your life, what you will eat or drink; or about your body, what you will wear. . . . Your heavenly Father knows that you need them" (Matthew 6:25, 32). This was Peter's point in assuring his readers of God's care: "Cast all your anxiety on him because he cares for you" (1 Peter 5:7; see also Philippians 4:6–7).

It makes sense that God cares for those individuals who have trusted in Jesus and are therefore accepted by God, but does God care about unbelievers, sinners, those who have rejected his Son? Jesus answers this question in Luke 15:3–7 through a story about a shepherd who leaves ninety-nine sheep that are safe to search for one sheep that is lost. When he finds it, he rejoices. Jesus concludes, "I tell you that in the same way there will be more rejoicing in heaven over one sinner who repents than over ninety-nine righteous persons who do not need to repent" (v. 7). This love of God for the individual in need of salvation explains why, while Philip was successfully spreading the gospel among the Samaritans (Acts 8:4–8), God directed him to go to the middle of nowhere and talk to one man, an Ethiopian eunuch, who needed to know about Jesus Christ (Acts 8:26–35). As a result, that one man believed and was baptized (vv. 36–40).

But the greatest evidence that God cares for all individuals is the fact that he sent his Son to die in the place of each of us in order to meet the greatest need any of us have, and that is to be forgiven and made right with him (Romans 5:6–8; 2 Corinthians 5:21; 1 Peter 3:18; 1 John 4:10).

FAMILY FACT

Even though it may seem strange to us, God cares so much for his children that he lovingly disciplines or corrects them. "The Lord disciplines those he loves, as a father the son he delights in" (Proverbs 3:12, quoted in Hebrews 12:6). So if you are a child of God through Jesus Christ (John 1:12) and are being disciplined by God, take it as an indication of his Fatherly love, not his anger. This is why the previous verse in Proverbs 3 says, "My son, do not despise the Lord's discipline, and do not resent his rebuke" (v. 11). Why? Because God does it for your good (Hebrews 12:10–11).

Are We Expected to Obey the Laws of the Old Testament?

The relationship between the Old Testament Law and the Christian is a surprisingly complex issue. Not everyone understands it in the same way. Let me suggest what I think is a safe, commonsense approach (acknowledging that much more could be said).

First, the laws in the Old Testament essentially reflect the holy nature of God himself. This principle is found within the Law: "I am the LORD your God; consecrate yourselves and be holy, because I am holy" (Leviticus 11:44, repeated in vv. 45; 19:2; 20:7–8). Because God's nature does not change, this principle does not change, and therefore it is repeated in the New Testament: "But just as he who called you is holy, so be holy in all you do; for it is written: 'Be holy, because I am holy'" (1 Peter 1:15–16). Just as Old Testament Israel was called by a holy God and therefore expected to reflect his holy character, so New Testament Christians are called by a holy God, who rightfully expects the same thing from us.

Second, the essence of the Old Testament Law is summarized by Jesus in Matthew 22:36–40. Jesus answered the question about which law is the greatest by quoting from the Law itself, "'Love the Lord your God with all your heart and with all your soul and with all your mind' [Deuteronomy 6:5]. This is the first and greatest commandment. And the second is like it: 'Love your neighbor as yourself' [Leviticus 19:18]. All the Law and the Prophets hang on these two commandments." Not only the Law, but the ethic of the entire Old Testament is summarized by these two commandments: Love God and love others. The spirit of the Old Testament Law clearly still applies to Christians (Romans 13:8–10; Galatians 5:14; James 2:8). Love for God and love for others are explicitly tied together in 1 John 4:7–21. Verse 21 says, "Anyone who loves God must also love their brother or sister."

Third, Christians are by no means expected to keep many of the laws in the Old Testament. The most obvious examples are the laws regarding animal sacrifices. Those have been rendered unnecessary because of the final, perfect sacrifice of Jesus himself (Hebrews 9:11–14). The clean and unclean food laws are also irrelevant to New Testament Christians. Jesus said, "Don't you see that nothing that enters a person from the outside can defile them? For it doesn't go into their heart but into their stomach, and then out of the body" (Mark 7:18–19). The gospel writer immediately adds, "In saying this, Jesus declared all foods clean" (v. 19; see also Acts 10:9–15). Most of the specific laws of the Old Testament are understood by all to be no longer binding on Christians.

Fourth, Paul says several times that we, as Christians, are no longer under the law (Romans 6:14; 7:4–6; Galatians 3:24–26) because Christ has put an end to it (Romans 10:4). What Paul seems to have in mind here (although this is much debated) is that Christians are "new covenant" people, not "old covenant" people. The old covenant refers to the law, which could only condemn and never save (Romans 3:20; 4:15; 8:3; Galatians 2:17; Hebrews 7:18–19;

10:1). This does not mean that the law is bad or a failure; rather, it is good and holy (Romans 7:12, 22). But God never intended the law to be a way of salvation, but rather a way to make clear to sinners that they need salvation and a savior (Romans 3:20; 7:7; Galatians 3:19–26; 1 Timothy 1:8–9). The new covenant is based upon and initiated by the death and resurrection of Jesus Christ, and it replaced the old covenant (Hebrews 8:6–13). So since the many specific laws found in the Old Testament were all a part of the old covenant, the Mosaic Law, it seems that those laws no longer directly apply to Christians. The old covenant is obsolete and Christians are not a part of that covenant.

If Christians are not under the law, does that mean there are no laws to abide by? If we are saved by grace, does that mean we can live any way we want to? Paul answers that in no uncertain terms: "What then? Shall we sin because we are not under the law but under grace? By no means!" (Romans 6:15). Rather, Christians are repeatedly called to obedience (Titus 3:1; 1 Peter 1:14; 2 John 1:6), and there are many specific commands in the New Testament that obviously directly apply to Christians. Some of these reflect Old Testament laws, because God's holy nature has not changed. For example, discussing love as the fulfillment of the law (Romans 13:8–10), Paul specifically mentions four of the Ten Commandments: "You shall not commit adultery"; "You shall not murder"; "You shall not steal"; "You shall not covet" (v. 9). He goes on to say that love for one's neighbor fulfills these specific commands. In Ephesians 6:1–2, Paul tells children to obey their parents and then quotes the fourth commandment as the foundation: "Honor your father and mother" [Exodus 20:12]. Another of the Ten Commandments is "You shall not give false testimony against your neighbor" (Exodus 20:16). This essentially means that God's people are to love truth and treat others with integrity, honesty, and justice, which the New Testament often commands of Christians (1 Corinthians 13:6; Ephesians 4:25; Colossians 3:9;

2 John 4; 3 John 3–4). Obviously, the New Testament is filled with restatements and reapplications of the first three of the Ten Commandments regarding serving and worshiping God alone (John 4:23–24; Romans 12:1; 1 Corinthians 10:31; James 4:7–8; 1 John 5:2) and having nothing to do with idols (1 Corinthians 10:7, 14; Colossians 3:5).

In summary, God has not changed from the Old Testament to the New Testament, and therefore, he still calls his people to be holy as he is holy. The laws of the New Testament reflect this just as the laws of the Old Testament do. So despite the complexity of trying to figure out exactly how Old Testament laws apply to New Testament Christians, we can be assured that as we follow New Testament commands applied directly to New Testament Christians *in dependence upon God*, we will be doing what God wants us to do. We will take this up further in the next chapter.

FUN FACT

It seems clear that Christians are no longer under the Law of Moses, but we are under "Christ's law" (1 Corinthians 9:21; Galatians 6:2). These aren't different sets of laws; rather, the Law of Moses only anticipated the law of Christ, whereas the law of Christ supersedes the Law of Moses. The law of Christ is superior to the Law of Moses in that it not only makes divine demands but also supplies the power through the Holy Spirit to obey those demands (Romans 8:1–14; Galatians 5:16–25). That's something the Old Testament laws could never do.

36

Where in the Bible Can I Learn About How God Wants Me to Live?

Throughout the Bible God tells us how he wants us to live, which we call ethics or morality. The first command appears in the very first chapter—"Be fruitful and increase" (Genesis 1:28). The first prohibition comes in the next chapter—"You must not eat from the tree of the knowledge of good and evil" (Genesis 2:17). In the latter part of the Old Testament, God continued to remind his people through the prophets to keep his laws, such as Malachi, in the very last chapter of the Old Testament: "Remember the law of my servant Moses, the decrees and laws I gave him" (4:4).

As we saw in the previous chapter, even though many of the specific laws in the Old Testament do not directly apply to Christians, God's character is revealed in all of those laws, and God requires that we be conformed to his holy character (1 Peter 1:15). We also saw that many of the Old Testament laws are repeated and reapplied in the New Testament.

The Old Testament also contains both positive and negative examples of how God wants us to live. Paul recognized this when he reviewed historical events after the exodus and told his readers, "Now these things occurred as examples to keep us from setting our hearts on evil things as they did" (1 Corinthians 10:6; see also verse 11). A negative example is Israel's continual rebellion and idolatry. On the other hand, positive examples include Moses, who was called a friend of God (Exodus 33:11), and David, who was called a man after God's own heart (1 Samuel 13:14; Acts 13:22). We can study their lives to find out how they achieved these honorary titles.

The Proverbs are also an excellent Old Testament source for finding out how God wants us to live. The biblical proverbs are, by definition, practical advice for living in a way that God considers a success. This is the goal of biblical wisdom and is based on the "fear of [or reverence for] the LORD" (1:7; 9:10). A very important point here is that we cannot live in the right way unless we understand God in the right way. Once again, we see how crucial the holiness of God is in shaping our own ethics.

In the Gospels, Jesus taught us how to live, such as in the Sermon on the Mount (Matthew 5:3–7:27). But he did more than *teach* us how to live, he *showed* us. In fact, he came to fulfill the law (Matthew 5:17). He was the only human who ever lived who was able to do this, and therefore he modeled for the rest of us perfect obedience to God. He provided an example of a humble, servant attitude (John 13:15–17), and even showed us how to be willing to suffer and even die for him (Matthew 16:24–27; 1 Peter 2:21–24). The bottom line is: "Whoever claims to live in him must live as Jesus did" (1 John 2:6).

The letters of the New Testament often focus on Christian ethics. It was the specific purpose of these writers to teach Christians what to believe (theology) and how to live as a result (ethics). Paul structured his letters in this important order. For example, in Ephesians 4:1, he wrote, "I urge you to live a life worthy of the calling you have received." In the previous chapters, he described that calling (being "in Christ"), and at this point he applies it to their lives. This includes practicing humility, gentleness, patience, and unity, as he notes in the subsequent verses. We should consider the commands, prohibitions, and exhortations in the Epistles as equal in authority to those of Jesus himself, since he delegated his authority to the apostles.

Whenever we are considering ethical issues—how we ought to live—we must be careful to stay biblically balanced so we don't slip into legalism. That is, we must always fight the tendency to think and act as if our relationship with God depends on how well we can impress him with what we do and how we live. Instead, we must realize that what pleases God is our faith or dependence upon him (Hebrews 11:6). This is true both for becoming a Christian in the first place as well as living as a Christian for the rest of our lives. It is *all* by God's grace that we receive by faith (Ephesians 2:8–9). This should be obvious when we consider the ethical standard that Jesus set in the Sermon on the Mount: "Be perfect, therefore, as your heavenly Father is perfect" (Matthew 5:48). The standard could not be higher; moral perfection is what God demands. But we cannot meet that demand apart from dependence upon God himself. This does not mean that how we live is unimportant or irrelevant. Christians are called to produce good works, not in order to persuade God to accept them, but because God has *already* accepted them (Ephesians 2:10; Titus 2:14; James 2:14–26). What pleases God, then, is that the good works that we do are done in dependence upon him, not to impress him.

Closely related to this is the idea that we should do what we do before God with the right heart, that is, the right motives, thoughts, and attitudes (1 Samuel 16:7; 1 Chronicles 28:9; Proverbs 16:2; Matthew 5:28; 15:18–20; 1 Corinthians 4:5). *What* we do is important, but what is more important is *why* we do it. This is why

Jesus criticized the Pharisees for doing "good" things like giving money to the poor, praying, and fasting. They were not doing it for God's approval, but for man's (Matthew 6:1–17; Luke 16:15).

What are proper motives for what we do? Two clearly stand out in the Bible. First, we should do what we do in order to glorify God, not ourselves (Matthew 6:16; John 15:8; 1 Corinthians 10:31). Second, we should do what we do out of love (1 Corinthians 13:1–3). Jesus clearly stressed the connection between love for him and obedience to him: "If you love me, keep my commands" (John 14:15; see also vv. 21, 23; 15:10; 1 John 5:3). One of those commands is to "love each other as I have loved you" (John 15:12; 1 John 3:11–24; 4:11–12, 19–21). So we should be motivated by our love for God as well as our love for others.

How do we please God by what we do and how we live? By doing everything in dependence upon him. He has provided the help we need to do the impossible—to be holy as he is holy. That help comes from the Holy Spirit, who lives inside those who have believed in Christ (Romans 8:4–17; Galatians 5:16–25). Furthermore, we please God when we do everything out of love for the purpose of glorifying him.

FUN FACT

Augustine wisely said in his book *Confessions,* "Give what you command, and command what you will."[1] God has commanded that we be ethically perfect. But we do not despair as a result of that lofty demand. Rather, we rejoice in knowing that he has also given what he commands—through his Son, who provides forgiveness for sin, and through his Spirit, who provides strength for obedience.

Is It Good to Have a Plan for Reading the Bible?

The Word of God is essential to our spiritual lives, both in coming to know God in the first place and as we continue to grow in our faith. First Peter 1:23 says, "For you have been born again, not of perishable seed, but of imperishable, through the living and enduring word of God." In other words, the Word of God plays a vital role in our becoming Christians. But to those who have been born again, Peter adds, "Like newborn babies, crave pure spiritual milk, so that by it you may grow up in your salvation" (1 Peter 2:2). Just as babies need nourishment to grow and thrive physically, so Christians need spiritual nourishment to grow and thrive spiritually. Peter is not only talking to new or "baby" Christians; he is telling everyone who has been born again to crave the Word of God like babies crave milk.

Although Peter is *not* distinguishing between new and old or mature and immature Christians, the writer of Hebrews *does* make that distinction when he writes, "In fact, though by this time you ought to be teachers, you need someone to teach you the elementary truths of God's word all over again. You need milk, not solid food! Anyone who lives on milk, being still an infant, is not acquainted with the teaching about righteousness. But solid food is for the mature, who by constant use have trained themselves to distinguish good from evil" (Hebrews 5:12–14). This author is disappointed with his readers. They have been Christians long enough that they should not only know the deep things of the Word of God (solid food) but be teaching them to others. But instead, they are stuck in immaturity and still need baby food (milk). Who are the mature? Those "who by constant use [of God's Word] have trained themselves to distinguish good from evil" (v. 14). It could not be clearer: We cannot become Christians without the truth found in the Bible, nor can we become mature, holy Christians without the Bible. It is an essential part of our spiritual diet. We need to feed constantly on Scripture.

This is what Jesus meant when he said, "Man shall not live on bread alone, but on every word that comes from the mouth of God" (Matthew 4:4). Jesus said this while being tempted by Satan; he quoted Deuteronomy 8:3 to protect himself spiritually. In other words, even Jesus himself needed to be strengthened by God's Word. At the last supper, Jesus prayed on behalf of his followers and requested of his Father, "Sanctify them [or make them holy] by the truth; your word is truth" (John 17:17).

So in the same way that we plan for things that are vital for our well-being in other areas—eating, exercise, finances—we also need to plan to regularly feed on the Word of God. If we are honest, we will admit that if we don't make a plan, we probably won't do it. So, should we plan to read the Bible? Absolutely! Our spiritual health is at stake!

Here is my challenge to you: commit to reading through the entire Bible regularly—every year or two. That may sound over-whelming, but it is not too hard if you have a plan. Reading the entire Bible is important because the entire Bible is important. God does not waste words on unimportant things. So our goal should be to get God's Word into us over and over again throughout our lives.

There are many good plans available to help you. Back to the Bible has a variety of reading schedules to meet many needs at backtothebible.org: You can read through the Bible from beginning to end in the order of the canon (the order found in your Bible). You can read through the Bible chronologically, that is, reading the books in the order in which they fit in the flow of biblical history. You can read through the Old Testament and New Testament simultaneously. They also offer a plan that blends some of these strategies.

Some study Bibles include reading schedules. For example, the English Standard Version Study Bible has one that covers the entire Bible in one year. Assignments for each day include passages from four categories: Psalms and Wisdom Literature; Pentateuch and the History of Israel; Chronicles and Prophets; and Gospels and Epistles. (If you have an English Standard Version Study Bible, you can find this on pages 2743–2750.)

You can even devise your own schedule. There are 929 chapters in the Old Testament and 260 chapters in the New Testament. If you want to read each day, divide the total by 365. It might be wise to allow some flexibility in your schedule and set a goal for reading the Bible twenty-five days each month; that would mean dividing the total chapters by 300. If you want to move a bit slower, divide the chapters by 600 and cover the Bible in two years, reading twenty-five days per month.

I would encourage you to change things up along the way. Variety brings freshness, which is especially important if this is something you want to do for the rest of your life. Doing the same thing over and over can become routine and boring. For example, for your first read-through, start at Genesis and keep going until you reach the end of Revelation. Next time, read the books of the Bible chronologically. There have been several occasions when, due to my own spiritual needs, I have decided to read through and meditate on the psalms exclusively (regarding meditation, see chapter 39). I would read the book of Psalms two to three times in a year. But then, I would complete the rest of the Bible in the next year so that, over a two-year span, I had read the entire Bible. As is so important with any spiritual discipline, such as Bible reading, memorization, and meditation, find out what works for you and do that.

Remember one of the key texts regarding the inspiration of Scripture. Second Timothy 3:16 says, "All Scripture is God-breathed . . ." The next verse provides the purpose: ". . . so that the servant of God may be thoroughly equipped for every good work" (v. 17). Through our commitment to regularly reading and studying the Bible, God will accomplish this wonderful purpose in our lives.

FUN FACT

My wife, Marilyn, committed to reading through the Bible regularly soon after we were married. She has kept with it, and now, some thirty years later, she would wholeheartedly join me in commending this commitment to you as one that will provide rich spiritual blessings. In other words, you don't have to be a pastor or a Bible professor to make this kind of commitment!

Is It Essential to
Memorize Scripture?

Getting God's Word into our hearts and minds is essential for spiritual health. Two disciplines that can aid us in this process are memorizing, and meditating on, biblical texts. In this chapter, we will consider memorization, and in the next chapter, meditation.

Memorization is a way to get the Word of God off the pages of the Bible and into our lives for the long haul. We can have a whole shelf full of Bibles, but they do us no good until we know what is in them; so of course we need to read the Bible. But how much better is it to get Scripture into our minds in such a way that it stays there far beyond the time spent reading the Bible and maybe for a few moments afterward. When we memorize Scripture, God can use it whenever he wishes to help us, encourage us, convict us, and challenge us. The written Word of God came through the Holy Spirit's work of inspiration (2 Peter 1:21), so it makes sense that if we get the Word into our memory banks, the Spirit will work through it to guide us into truth (John 16:13) and guide us into his way of living (Galatians 5:16–25).

One of the greatest benefits of memorizing Scripture is stated in Psalm 119:11: "I have hidden your word in my heart that I might not sin against you." In every case, when Jesus was being tempted by Satan, he responded by quoting Scripture (Matthew 4:1–11; he quoted from Deuteronomy!). Since Jesus is God of the universe, he could have simply commanded Satan to leave him alone and Satan would have had to submit. But instead, Jesus provided a model for us regarding how to deal with temptation: use the Word of God. We are promised that if we submit to God and then resist the devil, he will flee from us (James 4:7). What better way to resist Satan than by the Word of God (Ephesians 6:10–18, especially verse 17, which tells us to stand against the devil with "the sword of the Spirit, which is the word of God").

There are many other benefits of memorizing Scripture. In the next chapter we will see a few more when memorization is combined with meditation. And in the final chapter we will see how the Bible, and specifically memorizing it, can help us to pray (John 15:7).

Here are some practical suggestions for memorizing biblical texts:

1. Acknowledge how vital the Bible is to your spiritual health and crave it as a baby craves milk (1 Peter 2:2). Ask God to increase this craving. This will provide the motivation to undertake and keep up this challenging discipline.

2. Choose passages to memorize that are the most important to you spiritually and emotionally. As you are reading through the Bible, list verses that you find challenging, helpful, and encouraging, and start memorizing them. For example, if you struggle with anxiety,

memorize Matthew 6:33–34 or Philippians 4:6. If you find it hard just to trust God, memorize Psalm 37:3–5 or Proverbs 3:5. An effective system known as the *Topical Memory System* has been developed by the Navigators (Navigators.org). It includes sixty verses that lay a good biblical foundation for newer Christians.

3. Study the passages. Knowing what they mean in their contexts will help you remember them and apply them.

4. Experiment with recognized techniques of memorization, such as imagery or mental association. There are countless books in stores and online that can help you develop these and other techniques.

5. Review what you have memorized. This is necessary for long-term mental retrieval of what has been memorized.

6. Develop a system for memorization and review. Many people find it helpful to write the passage they want to memorize on a card. Carry the card with you and review it periodically throughout the day. Use moments in your day that would otherwise be wasted, such as while you are standing in line, waiting for an appointment, or sitting at a stoplight. You will be amazed at how productive these brief times can be.

7. Set realistic goals—maybe one verse a week to begin with. As with physical exercise or weight loss, setting one's goals too high is almost a certain guarantee of failure.

8. Memorize verses from the translation that you use most and are most familiar with. The wording of these verses will be most familiar to you, and as you read the Bible,

you will also be reviewing the verses you have memorized. As an alternative, check the wording of a verse that you want to memorize from a number of translations and memorize the translation that is clearest and most meaningful to you.

9. Give it a try. Too many people don't even try because they assume they are not good at memorization. Some people have amazing abilities to memorize; most of us don't. But we can all memorize to some degree.

10. Challenge yourself. After you get used to memorizing a verse or two, try memorizing a whole paragraph, chapter, or maybe even a short book.

11. Be humble. As with all good things, there are dangers. One danger here is spiritual pride ("Do you know how much of the Bible I have memorized?"). The Pharisees knew the Jewish Scriptures well and had memorized large portions of it, and yet Jesus often criticized them for their pride and doing things to be noticed by men (Matthew 6:1). Memorizing the Word of God does not guarantee that it will have a good effect upon our lives. We need to do it with the right attitude of humility, dependence upon God, and a true desire to honor God rather than ourselves.

FUN FACT

Dawson Trotman was a troubled young man who agreed to start attending church rather than go to jail. He accepted a challenge at the church and memorized twenty verses. One day as he was on his way to work, one of the verses that he memorized, John 5:24, popped into his consciousness: "Verily, verily, I say unto you, He that heareth my word, and believeth on him that sent me, hath everlasting life" (KJV). After that, another verse (John 1:12) came to mind. As a result, Trotman trusted in Christ and became a Christian. During the rest of his life, he memorized hundreds of verses from the Bible, founded a very successful Christian organization, the Navigators, and taught thousands of others how to memorize Scripture.

How Do I Meditate on the Word of God?

Along with memorization, meditation is an excellent way to activate the power of God's Word in our lives. The idea in both is to internalize Scripture so that the Holy Spirit can work through it to guide us, teach us, and purify us.

There are more explicit references to meditation in the Bible than to memorization, probably because meditation usually assumes memorization. In Joshua 1:8, we hear God himself command meditation and explain its benefit: "Keep this Book of the Law always on your lips; meditate on it day and night, so that you may be careful to do everything written in it. Then you will be prosperous and successful." In the context, the benefits are *not* that Joshua will be rich and famous, but rather that he will be obedient to God's commands and successfully complete what God called him to do—that is, he will be successful in God's eyes.

The writers of the psalms also practiced meditation. The book of Psalms begins like this: "Blessed is the one who does not walk in step with the wicked or stand in the way that sinners take or sit in the company of mockers, but whose delight is in the law of the LORD, and who meditates on his law day and night" (Psalm 1:1–2). In the NIV translation of Psalm 119, there are eight references to meditation. For example, "I meditate on your precepts and consider your ways" (Psalm 119:15). Later, in the same psalm, the psalmist wrote, "Oh, how I love your law! I meditate on it all day long" (Psalm 119:97). The psalm continues by noting several benefits of meditation: "Your commands are always with me and make me wiser than my enemies. I have more insight than all my teachers, for I meditate on your statutes" (vv. 98–99). The benefits here are wisdom and insight. The Hebrew word used for *meditate* in the psalms means to "talk to oneself," implying mental activities such as contemplating, pondering, considering, remembering, and reflecting upon.

The concept of meditation can be seen in the New Testament in Philippians 4:8: "Finally, brothers and sisters, whatever is true, whatever is noble, whatever is right, whatever is pure, whatever is lovely, whatever is admirable—if anything is excellent or praiseworthy—think about [meditate upon, reflect upon, ponder, consider] such things." A similar idea is found in Colossians 3:16: "Let the message of Christ dwell among you richly."

Meditation is something that happens inside of us, in our *heart,* to use the biblical term (Psalm 19:14), that is, within our thoughts and spirit. So with regard to Scripture, meditation simply means thinking about or reflecting on it. We read and memorize Scripture to get it into our minds, but then it is important that we meditate on it to take us deeper into understanding it and applying it to our lives. In contrast to other forms of mediation, such as Eastern or Transcendental Meditation, this is not the act of emptying one's mind of all thoughts, but rather of filling one's mind with God's Word.

Let me suggest some basic principles to get you started on biblical meditation.

1. Set aside adequate time and space. Fruitful meditation cannot be rushed. Choose a time when interruptions and distractions are minimal, if not avoided altogether. If at all possible, the beginning of the day is good because you can then continue to carry the benefits of your meditation with you throughout the day. Choose a place where you can be alone and other responsibilities of the day will not divert your attention.

2. Choose a biblical word, phrase, or verse as the focus of your meditation. As with verses you choose to memorize, these should meet a particular need you have (for comfort, trust, encouragement, challenge). Keep the section of Scripture small in order to concentrate your focus. Ideally, you should have memorized the text, or you can memorize it as you meditate on it.

3. Begin with prayer. Ask God to work in your thinking during your time of meditation. Ask him to reveal himself to you and to draw you closer to him. Ask him to open your eyes to the truth that is in his Word. Ask him to help you apply his Word to your life. Ask him to transform you through meditation on his Word.

4. Think about the meaning of the text. It would be helpful to have studied the text before your time of meditation so that you have a general understanding of it. During your meditation, then, your goal is to go deeper in that understanding and to have your eyes opened to things that you had not seen or understood before. What is God saying through the text? Why is it important?

5. Think about application of the text. In what practical ways can you apply that biblical truth to your life immediately?

6. Write down your thoughts regarding meaning and application. Jot down questions regarding the text that may take additional study and thought to answer.

7. End your time with prayer. Thank God for his presence and ask him to help you apply his Truth to your life as you go through the day.

Read a few of the many good books that offer practical advice for meditating on Scripture. As with other disciplines, such as Bible reading and memorization, be creative, experiment, and come up with something that works for you.

As in all things, do this in humility and dependence upon God. You do not earn points with God by meditating. Rather, you put yourself in a place where God can do significant things in your life. Meditation is not easy, but the spiritual benefits of this discipline are well worth it.

FUN FACT

When I was a pastor and regularly preparing sermons, the greatest challenge was usually the application—how was the biblical text relevant to the people in my church? When I would get stuck, I would practice what I call "sit and stare time." I would go to a coffee shop, stare out the window, and think. It was essentially a time of meditation on the text of my sermon. I cannot think of a time when God did not faithfully use that meditation to bring thoughts to my mind with regard to application of his Word. Try it yourself. See how God may be pleased to meet with you and do amazing things through your time of meditation on his Word.

Is It a Good Idea to Use the Bible When I Pray?

We have already mentioned how important communication is to any relationship. To have a healthy relationship with God, we need to have healthy communication with him. The Bible is a part of this communication with God; it is God speaking to us. The God-given means for our communicating with him is prayer. So Bible reading and prayer should go together: God speaks to us through his written Word, and we respond through prayer. In fact, we are commanded in Scripture to pray (Philippians 4:6), and more than that, to "pray without ceasing" (1 Thessalonians 5:17 NASB). This is because God knows how vital prayer is to our spiritual health.

Because prayer is so important, God has provided models for prayer in the Bible. The most obvious and best known is the Lord's Prayer in Matthew 6:9–13 and Luke 11:1–4. The latter reference is Jesus' direct response to his disciples' request that he teach them to pray. So I would certainly recommend this prayer model to you, but since it is covered so well in so many other sources, I would like to draw your attention to a few other prayers in the Bible that are also worth imitating.

One example that might not immediately seem like a model for prayer is found in Genesis 32:22–32. This passage tells about a strange event in the life of Jacob in which he finds himself wrestling with a mysterious person late at night. This person demands to be let go, but Jacob says, "I will not let you go unless you bless me" (v. 26). In response, the man changed Jacob's name to Israel. Why? "Because you have struggled with God and with humans and have overcome" (v. 28). *Israel* means "he struggles with God," or essentially, "God-wrestler." It turns out that Jacob was wrestling with none other than God himself, which he indicates by naming the location Peniel, which means "I saw God face-to-face" (v. 30). But also note that God granted Jacob's request for a blessing (v. 29). I believe this is a model for prayer in the sense that God wants us to come into his presence (now, through Jesus Christ), "wrestle" with him in faith, and seek his blessing. God desires this because he loves us and wants the best for us, and the best certainly includes his blessing. God is honored by this because it is our way of acknowledging that he alone is the source of highest blessing, and that we will not settle for anything less. The prayer of Jabez, in 1 Chronicles 4:10, is another illustration of this.

Moses provides two more models that show us how to use the Bible in our prayers. The first is in Exodus 32:11–13. God had just told Moses that he intended to judge Israel because they were worshiping the golden calf idol. Moses prayed that God would forgive them. In the prayer, Moses said, "Remember your servants Abraham, Isaac and Israel [Jacob's new name], to whom you swore by your own self: 'I will make your descendants as numerous as the stars in the sky and I will give your descendants all this land I promised them, and it will be their inheritance forever'" (v. 13). Of course God had not forgotten his promise, but the important thing is that Moses had not forgotten God's promise either. The promise to which Moses appeals is the Abrahamic covenant. Moses was "wrestling" with God on behalf of the people of Israel and making a request of God *based upon God's own promises*. Our lesson is that we, too, should pray based upon the promises of God. Where do we find those promises? In the Bible. So know what God has promised you in the Bible and then ask him to do what he has already promised. God doesn't need reminders, but it is important for us to know and remember God's promises and base our prayer requests on them.

The second example from Moses is in Numbers 14:13–19. The situation is the same: God planned to judge his rebellious people. Again, Moses wrestled with God on their behalf. Note the basis for Moses' request for forgiveness this time: "Now may the Lord's strength be displayed, just as you have declared: 'The LORD is slow to anger, abounding in love and forgiving sin and rebellion. Yet he does not leave the guilty unpunished; he punishes the children for the sin of the parents to the third and fourth generation.' In accordance with your great love, forgive the sin of these people" (vv. 17–19). The request is *based now upon God's own character*, specifically his love. Moses even quoted God's own description of himself back to God—"The LORD is slow to anger, abounding in love and forgiving" (Numbers 14:18). Moses' request boils down to "God, forgive your people because you are a forgiving God." The lesson here is to pray prayers based on the character of God. Where do we find this? In the Bible. So know who God is from the Bible and make your prayer requests in keeping with his character.

A few other great models for prayer in Scripture include Ezra's prayer in Ezra 9:5–15; Nehemiah's prayers in Nehemiah 1:4–11; the Levites' prayer in Nehemiah 9:5–38; and Daniel's prayer in Daniel 9:3–19. Observe how they worship God in prayer. This is important because it reminds us of our great God and that we can have confidence in him as we bring our requests to him. Also observe their humility and confession of sin. This should remind us of our sinfulness, weakness, and need. That is why we are coming to God in prayer. These together illustrate the proper perspective we should have in prayer toward God and ourselves. Study Paul's prayers in 1 Thessalonians 3:11–13; Ephesians 1:15–19; and Colossians 1:9–14. Observe what Paul prays for, and pray for the same kinds of things. Finally, use the psalms, which are great models for prayer. Relate to and identify with the emotions evident in the psalms—from praise, exultation, joy, and thankfulness, all the way to anger, frustration, sorrow, fear, loneliness, and humiliation. All our emotions can be found here. Then make these psalms your own. Let them help you express your own emotions in humble, trusting honesty to God, for the sake of a healthy relationship with him.

God delights in his own Word, and therefore he also delights when we use his Word in our prayers.

FUN FACT

It is significant that Jesus prayed so much, sometimes for an entire night (Luke 6:12). Why? After all, he himself is God. A part of the answer is that he is also human. In his humanity, he has modeled for us our need of God and therefore our need of prayer.

Notes

Chapter 1: Why Should I Read the Bible?

1. This well-known phrase comes from the *Westminster Shorter Catechism* in answer to the first question: "What is the chief end of man?" This influential document was produced in the 1640s during the English Reformation period.

Chapter 4: What Is the Main Theme of the Bible?

1. Credit for this terminology and idea goes to a former professor of mine, Duane Litfin, *Conceiving the Christian College* (Grand Rapids: Eerdmans, 2004), chap. 3.

Chapter 14: How Is the New Testament Organized?

1. Bruce Metzger, *The Text of the New Testament* (Oxford: Oxford University Press, 1968), 205.

Chapter 22: In What Languages Was the Bible Written?

1. Norman Geisler and William E. Nix, *A General Introduction to the Bible* (Chicago: Moody Press, 1968), 220.

Chapter 25: What Do We Mean When We Say the Bible Is the Word of God?

1. The Qur'an is the book composed of writings accepted by Muslims as revelations made to Muhammad by Allah and as the divinely authorized basis for the religious, social, civil, commercial, military, and legal regulations of the Islamic world.

Chapter 26: What Internal Evidence Do We Have That the Bible Is the Word of God?

1. Peter W. Stone, *Science Speaks*, 3rd rev. ed. (Chicago: Moody Press, 1969).
2. Ibid., 111.
3. Frank Morison, *Who Moved the Stone?* (Grand Rapids: Zondervan, 1987).

Chapter 28: Why Does It Matter That the Bible Is the Word of God?

1. Often in the Old Testament, the Hebrew word *elohim* refers to God himself. In Psalm 82, however, it is used in verses 1 and 6 of human rulers or judges under the absolute rule and judgment of God himself (*elohim* is used in this same way in Exodus 22:8-9 and Psalm 58:1). The point that Jesus is making in John 10:34-36 is, if human rulers can be called "gods," what is wrong with Jesus claiming to be the "Son of God," since he had been set apart and sent by God himself?

Chapter 29: Is All the History in the Bible Accurate?

1. Sir William Ramsey, *The Bearing of Recent Discovery on the Trustworthiness of the New Testament* (Grand Rapids: Baker, 1953).

2. Ramsey, *St. Paul the Traveler and the Roman Citizen* (Grand Rapids: Baker, 1962).

Chapter 32: What Do I Do When I Don't Understand What I'm Reading?

1. Probably the best explanation of this is available in Howard G. Hendricks and William D. Hendricks, *Living by the Book* (Chicago: Moody Press, 1991). Dr. Howard Hendricks is well known for being one of the most creative users and teachers of this method of Bible study.

Chapter 36: Where in the Bible Can I Learn About How God Wants Me to Live?

1. Saint Augustine of Hippo, *Confessions* (originally written in AD 397, it is a collection of thirteen books). Oxford World's Classics series, translated by Henry Chadwick (New York: Oxford University Press, 1998), book 10, chap. 29.

Daryl Aaron earned his MA at the University of Texas at Dallas, his ThM at Dallas Theological Seminary, his DMin at Bethel Theological Seminary, and his PhD at Graduate Theological Foundation. He spent fourteen years in pastoral ministry and now teaches at Northwestern College, where he is Professor of Biblical and Theological Studies. Dr. Aaron lives in Mounds View, Minnesota, with his wife, Marilyn. They have one daughter, Kimberly, who loves to study and teach Spanish.